FOR GENERATIONS TO COME

The Life Story of Elias Ingraham

FORREST M. HOLLY

FLEMING H. REVELL COMPANY
Old Tappan, New Jersey

Abridged from pp. 83-4 in THE TASTE MAKERS by Russell Lynes
Copyright 1954 by Russell Lynes
Reprinted by permission of Harper & Row Publishers, Inc.

Frontispiece: The "Ingraham" coat of arms as copied by Joan L. Ingraham from an old sewing box given her by Edward Ingraham II.

Library of Congress Cataloging in Publication Data

Holly, Forrest M
    For generations to come.

Includes index.
    1. Ingraham, Elias. I. Title.
TS544.8.I53H64   681'.113'0924 [B]   75-31669
ISBN 0-87653-026-9

Copyright © 1975 by Forrest M. Holly
Published by Fleming H. Revell Company, Old Tappan, N.J.
Printed in the United States of America

For Generations to Come

INGRAHAM

Contents

	Foreword	7
	Prologue	9
1	A Majority of One	15
2	Blossoms on the Family Tree	32
3	Up from the Sod	39
4	At the Master's Bench	47
5	The City that Could	54
6	Clocks Eclipse the Sun	62
7	Forever, My Love	70
8	Graceful Years of Aggrandizement	84
9	Bristol Clocks in Every Quarter	96
10	Bankruptcy!	109
11	Art Surrenders to Disciplined Hands	125
12	A Faithful Brother	132
13	The Purge of Fire	149
14	Thy Brother's Blood	162
15	Riding the Rails Westward	175
16	Harvest Years	187
17	The Pendulum Slows	196
18	Wingspread!	206
	Epilogue	217
	Index	219

Foreword

Distilling the life and times of a distinguished American industrialist into a book requires a special kind of perseverance. The research demands good eyes, a patient mind and streamlined organization.

The biographer of Elias Ingraham had the inspiration to begin this volume and the ambition to finish it. He resides in California—far from the sources of information needed to reconstruct the life of the famed clockmaker—so he sought the help of a great grandson of Elias Ingraham to help dig up the information needed. The recording, organizing and evaluating of the material is a separate story of no small dimensions.

I found many ways to help Forrest Holly but this is the California designer-builder's own story. He had to gather the threads, weave the cloth and fashion the garment. It is, I believe, a valuable reconstruction of a period now long passed and fast diminishing.

I commend the author for his noble efforts and achievements.

—Edward Ingraham
Bristol, Connecticut

Prologue

Following the graduation of our eldest son from Deerfield Academy a decade ago, my wife and I assembled with relatives in the lovely Tudor style brick home of my father-in-law, Morton C. Treadway of Bristol, Connecticut. At that gathering, Edward Ingraham II, my wife's maternal uncle now deceased, recounted to me stories of his great grandfather, Elias Ingraham—the best clock designer of 19th century America. Those yarns of Ingraham's courage, struggles, accomplishments and talent fired my ambition to prepare the biography of that venerable old Ingraham ancestor.

At the time I said nothing about my impulse, returning to California expecting my interest in the biography to wane. A month later my interest had not waned but waxed! What to do? How does a designer-builder and weekly newspaper columnist become a biographer?

Edward Ingraham II agreed to help. By mail from his home in Connecticut came the first of hundreds of documents upon which this work is based. So it was that the biography was eventually born, attended by the midwifery of a real New England gentleman, Edward Ingraham II. I am grateful for his patience, helpfulness and good cheer which have been so generously displayed over these past years of editorial collaboration.

Elias Ingraham was born in obscurity of devout, agrarian parents . . . disciplined by rugged custom and climate . . . gifted with native talent developed under a stern apprenticeship. His life spanned the careers of nineteen Presidents—beginning with Thomas Jefferson.

Red-headed, blue-green-eyed Elias Ingraham helped forge the industrial backbone of a young nation. Self-taught and self-made, he found his lifework, survived the birth throes of a new nation and that of his own business and gave to his family and community a heritage and clock company which have provided a livelihood for tens of thousands of families for more than a century and a third.

No man has contributed as much to the artistic design and the combination of beautiful forms in case making as he. Ingraham was not only a pioneer in the mass production of American clocks but from his indomitable energy, mechanical and artistic skill and business capabilities the Ingraham Company built a foundation that lasted for generations.

The Ingraham firm, one of America's oldest and most successful family companies, began in 1831. Andrew Jackson was in the White House; the railroad industry was booming; the first portents of differences which resulted in the Civil War 30 years later were appearing.

The company was managed successfully by five linear Ingraham generations before its corporate amalgamation in 1967.

After many years of extensive research the business of composing the manuscript began. It has been exciting, educational, poignant and sometimes frustrating. Through all the collateral books, articles, clippings and documents comes to light the career of an invincible Yankee clock-

Prologue

maker eminent in his profession, talented without an equal, courageous beyond the ordinary. His company was built so firmly that it survived and expanded while others withered and foundered.

Particularly worthy of note was Elias' purported trip to Caracas, Venezuela in the "roaring 1840s." Firm in family tradition, documented but once, this year-long sailing voyage to and from South America followed his bankruptcy of 1840. Some sixty years later material for a newspaper article was prepared by Elias' grandnephew, George Dudley Seymour of New Haven, an antiquarian, millionaire patent lawyer, historian of Nathan Hale, restorer of the Hale homestead. Mr. Seymour, trained by profession as a lawyer and by avocation as an historian, surely treated the truth with respect. It was he who described the voyage, declaring that the inspiration for the famous Sharp Gothic design came to Elias during the tedium of the long sailing voyage home.

In addition to readers interested in 19th century Industrial New England, this book is dedicated to Elias Ingraham's heirs, past, present and future, who to this day remain the beneficiaries of his remarkable achievements.

For thirty-one years I have happily lived with Elias' great-great-granddaughter, Jean Treadway Holly, my wife and the mother of our four, the great-great-great-grandchildren of Elias Ingraham. Though we personally knew him not, neither heard nor saw him, still we are the recipients of good which he generated in the bygone century.

With his original quaint misspelling, on Christmas Day, 1884, Elias Ingraham, nearly 80, with earthly shadows closing about him, summed up his cherished life hope in these prophetic words:

Now I Want this Clock Business to be kept and continued in the Hands and Harts of the Ingrahams Family for Many Generations to Come.

His dream has been fulfilled.

Lord God of Hosts, be with us yet,
Lest we forget—lest we forget!
—Rudyard Kipling

For Generations to Come

1

A Majority of One

Circa 1842-1843

Talent develops itself in solitude; character in the stream of life.

Red-headed Elias Ingraham had reached the first low point in his career that summer of 1840. Only two years earlier, just before President John Tyler's inauguration, bankruptcy had swallowed his clock and patent chair business. The nation's first industrial depression sapped him dry as a bone. He lost house and furnishings, shop, water privileges and clock and chair inventory, as well as comforts for his high-strung wife, Julia, and their ruddy young son Edward.

Ingraham was not alone. Other Bristol, Connecticut, businessmen, even those wiser and more affluent than he, had gone down the same moldering drain. It wasn't fun to be busted, to have the stigma of failure around. It was time for him to rouse, to act, and to venture. Had he not learned at the knee of his pietistic mother that the darkest hour precedes the dawn? Now was the time to prove it.

Julia was astonished that summer day when Elias came home and timidly called for his winter overcoat. Though she obediently carried it to her husband, she thought it a strange request. Why would her spouse want a winter coat on such a hot day?

Without another word or glance he turned from her, waved to his twelve-year-old son playing near the creek, abruptly strode down the tree-lined, dirt lane and vanished around the corner towards the tavern and stagecoach stop.

Where in the world is that man bound for? Julia wondered, stirring uneasily. She had no clue that her husband was off for a whole year and that she would have to take sole charge of keeping the boarders.

Climbing into a horse-drawn stage for New York, Elias Ingraham embarked that day on the first leg of his year-long sojourn in the velvet tropics of South America.

Why did he so unceremoniously run out on wife and son, hearth, home and village for so romantic a venture? Robust, resilient, in the prime of life, a tried and true businessman, family and church man, a bit melancholy by nature or circumstance, at thirty-seven Elias Ingraham had an inner itch that had to be scratched. And scratch it he did by sailing off for bizarre, remote Caracas, Venezuela. In the "roaring forties," Venezuela was about as far away as the moon, even to those more venturesome than the provincial Elias Ingraham.

He dreaded breaking the news to Julia that he was to sail off for a year. He knew she'd give him a hard time. What wife wouldn't?

The old Ingraham itch to dare, to do, to develop, flailed his "innards," hounding him without mercy. Fresh hope and a new impulse drove him to follow this day star rising within, a star hidden by the frustrations of recent financial failure. How could he tell Julia about it? In a letter, perhaps?

The stage rattled into New York. Elias Ingraham, plebeian, keen-eyed, strong, dignified but with little formal education, excitedly found his way to the bustling waterfront near The Battery. There, high-masted, graceful clipper ships, with carved pine figureheads at bows, even some of those new-fangled combination steam-driven sailing-packets, lay tied to berths, or swung at anchor chains chafed by tide or wind. To the cajoling of the mates, sweating, barefooted seamen wrestled lumber, soap, horses and mules, wine, fish, flour, and other commodities into holds under the watchful steel-blue eyes of the leather-faced captain on the quarterdeck. Elias smiled to see a milk cow, sheep, pigs, hens and ducks—travelers all—penned on the forward deck for commissary use by the ship's Chinese cook.

The era of Yankee clipper ships had just emerged. It was a time for iron men and wooden ships. Sailing vessels had barely begun to feel the pinch of steam-driven ships.

Elias inquired about sailings, probably sponsored by Howland & Aspenwall or B. Aymar & Co. A 300-ton wooden, copper-clad ship now due to slip away on the outgoing tide caught his blue-green eyes. This was the sailing ship that would carry him into the genial tropics for only $80 or $100. It would serve as a manger wherein would be born Elias Ingraham's clock child of the century, the exquisite Sharp Gothic.

Elias' conscience pricked him. He had not even properly said good-bye to dear Julia and little Edward. To break the news of his impending voyage to an overwrought wife before he left was not possible for him. She was a high-strung sort of woman. Such a confrontation might well have dissuaded him from his voyage.

Better to write her from New York, he told himself. And write her he did, a letter posted near The Battery that he was off to South America, winter overcoat and all.

The intelligence he dreaded to break face-to-face was now scrawled in longhand and posted for Bristol. Julia's sour reactions would be neither seen nor heard by her errant husband, but barbed they would be to her dying day.

That business comes before pleasure was Elias' shibboleth from Puritanic, agrarian ancestors. His trip was really not so capricious, although Julia, his stay-at-home, farm-bred wife, might reckon it so. He sought a wider market for his clocks and suitable sources of woods, like mahogany and rosewood for making clock cases. These considerations goaded him into the journey to South America.

Take Chauncey Jerome back there in Bristol. He had just shipped a consignment of Jerome mantel clocks to England. Had they not sold like hot cakes there? Were there not new orders from abroad for more Jerome clocks? Why, he'll make a mint! Should not he, Elias Ingraham, likewise pursue his own star? It might even now, like the Southern Cross, be rising in the south, in the West Indies or in that intriguing undercontinent South America.

The domestic clock market was still sluggish—all the more reason to seek wider markets for Yankee shelf clocks which he, Elias Ingraham, and his younger brother Andrew, could and did make with such care and success. He'd try to open markets for his clocks in every Caribbean port where the ship docked. Who knows! He might find in Havana, Port-au-Prince, Kingston or Caracas, Ingraham clock markets equal to those which Jerome had found in London. Why not? And when he returned with a new, foreign clock market, even though Julia might not forgive him for his long absence from home with that winter overcoat, at least she'd have to acknowledge the trip was profitable for his career. Then prosperity could again return to the Elias Ingrahams of Bristol.

Lines were cast off, the pilot taken aboard, sails unfurled and Elias Ingraham was on his way before a white, bubbly wake spreading aft. The ship, pretty as a picture, plowed its wooden way through the face of the deep, skimming along under thundering clouds of canvas. It bore southeast from Staten Island, set course past Sandy Hook, turned south ayont Hatteras, bowling along like a winged horse. With wind singing in the rigging, likely it sliced into the Gulf Stream blue, slid through Britain's Bahamas into Spain's Havana, crossed the Strait of Mona, boomed into Holland's Curacao, touched at Trinidad. League by tranquil league through the sultry Caribbean, Elias Ingraham had time to reflect, to dream, to think, to envision, even to listen to ship's bells. They reminded him of his beloved striking clocks. It was indeed a time to love.

The run of things had frustrated and disappointed him these last years. The business depression, his bankruptcy, endless legal maneuvers—all jaded his energy, choked his inventiveness, spiked his will to design new and beautiful clocks.

Far from the ordinary stream of life, dormant creativity began to resurface. He feasted his eyes on graceful hulls planked with oak or teakwood, tapering white pine masts, taut sails resembling a vast family laundry hung to dry, flying fish, sporting porpoises, noisy gulls, gliding pelicans, huge green turtles. He heard the creaking of blocks, the groan of straining hulls, the singing of taut shrouds, felt the cadence of mighty billows. The quiet rhythm of the ship plunging through warm, effervescent tropical waters wakened in Elias inspiration. It would presently burst into full activity.

Relieved for a time of the perplexities and routine of the work-a-day world, out from under the cloak flung over him by failure, Elias Ingraham was finding his daydreams refreshing, resuscitating, stimulating.

When did Elias sail to Caracas, Venezuela? Nobody knows for certain. Information as to his trip derives from a 1910 newspaper article reproduced later in this book. That his voyage was earlier rather than later in the roaring 1840s is substantiated by the author's research, especially concerning the Sharp Gothic clock which Elias designed on his return from South America.

Now preserved in the American Clock Museum at Bristol, Connecticut, is a Brewster and Ingraham's account book prepared by Andrew Ingraham, clockmaker and younger brother of Elias. It shows their first sale of the Sharp Gothic to be June, 1844. Thus we fix the time of Elias' one-year voyage to equatorial regions from the summer of 1842 to the summer of 1843. This would allow a year thereafter for Elias to develop working plans and begin manufacture of this famous clock style created during his South American trek.

Nineteenth century masters of vessels returning to United States' ports were required by law to deposit certified copies of their passenger lists with custom collectors at ports of entry. The New York list, admittedly incomplete through 1846, gives no reference to one Elias Ingraham.

Though legally not then required, passports from 1840 to 1850 in our National Archives have been examined, but no entry of Elias Ingraham is to be found.

Diplomatic dispatches were examined from the U.S. legation at Caracas and consular dispatches from La Guayra, as well as the National Archives of Venezuela, but they contain no reference to Elias Ingraham.

Polyglot Professor Walter Dupouy of Caracas, examining Venezuelan newspapers of 1842, found advertisements of European and American clocks, but no evidence of an Ingraham visit. Nor does Elias' name appear among those in the American colony in Venezuela during that period. Thus it may have been that his stay in Caracas was short.

"Land ho!" sang out from the crow's nest as Elias' ship moved southward. With pyramiding sails straining aloft, the ship careened along, trailed by an easterly breeze. Observe now Elias Ingraham, poised there on the sailing brig. It's only 7° to the equator. Below a candelabra of thunderheads he is approaching Cerro de Avila, the nearly 9000-foot-high precipitous South American mountainside. The ship skirts the palm-tree lined sea coast of Presidente Jose Antonio Paez's Venezuela.

See him scan with curious Yankee eyes the rather handsome Creole town of mostly one-story white houses with red tile roofs dotting the brick bat Cordillera de los Andes mountainside to 700 or 800 feet above the sea. The ship sloughs into its anchorage in the open roadstead off two and one-half-century-old La Guayra, the seaport for Caracas, with a temperature seldom below 82°.

From the sweltering shore he watches a swarthy port captain, a guard and an interpreter put out from the three-story, 150-foot-long, reddish, stone custom house cut into the mountainside. The official trio comes aboard to examine or clear cargo, crew and passengers. Elias' boxes of Bristol clocks ready to sell ashore are eyed with approval and interest by the black-moustachioed, tawny-skinned "El Capitan."

Now willing mulatto hands row Elias with his clocks to the 350-foot-long wooden mole resting on piles driven there in the sand. He springs ashore, likely the first Ingraham to feel South American soil underfoot. (The author, with his wife Jean T. Holly and her family—4th and 5th generation descendents of Elias Ingraham—visited La Guayra and Caracas during a 1966 Caribbean Cruise.)

He passes through a large gate. As a foreign traveler,

he presents himself to the mayor or chief magistrate and the military governor of La Guayra. They peer curiously, but politely, at his shock of red hair, his blue-green eyes, his imposing and dignified person. He gazes at these coffee-colored men, bronzed by tropical sun or otherwise pigmented in a multiplicity of colors by their mixture of Indian, Negro and European blood. It is said that the proportion of pure white to mixed blood is 1 to 100 or 1 to 200. He hears that scarcely a family is unconnected with either or both Indian or Negro blood.

Reminding Elias of his own well-watered New England, a cool mountain stream surges through the center of the populated parts of La Guayra. Originating thousands of feet above, the water turns into an underground canal, flows down the mountainside, rises at various points in stone reservoirs, spouts out from brick pillars.

Fronting the sea and the roadstead, there stretches a quarter-mile unbroken line of masonry, 18 to 24 feet high, 7 to 10 feet thick. (From a letter dated March 17, 1971, from Professor Walter Dupouy: "This is what is called a 'curtain,' term used for fortifications. La Guayra was a fortified town, and the old 'curtain' or fortified *front* still exists, although it cannot be seen from the town itself. Under or within these walls, were the prison cells named the 'Bovedas' (the vaults), where many of the republicans were imprisoned by the royalist army during the wars of independence, and after, vice-versa . . . . Of course, the public works and the growth of the port, probably destroyed part of these 'curtains' or *ramparts* of Colonial times. Still, I understand that some sections subsist underground and can be reached or have access only from the water side.") He is told it was built as a deterrent against Corsairs who plundered the West Indies until a few years back. La Guayra itself had once been a haven for smugglers . . . . Could so small and poor a city offer a wider market for clocks?

A Majority of One 23

Nearly 2,000 feet above, partially enveloped in cloud and mist, remindful of the colonial and pirate eras, on baked red soil he eyes old ruined fortifications, abandoned embrasures for cannons, and redoubts for sentry boxes.

He begs the interpreter to explain the reason for so many demolished buildings. He is told that the violent earthquake of 1812 killed 3,000 of some 6,000 inhabitants, that the city and fortifications were left in ruins, now only partly rebuilt. (The earthquake on Holy Thursday, 1812, wrought 20,000 casualties among 50,000 inhabitants of nearby Caracas.) Elias is struck with the widespread dilapidation of parts of the old city, one-third of which still lies in ruins. What a cataclysm that earthquake must have been!

Elias strides over 18-foot-wide, well-paved sidewalk-less streets. He examines some pretentious, flat, terraced-roofed houses with balconies evidencing the Basque influence. They show a good deal of style, with elegantly turned arches, windows without glass protected with iron bars. Plain fronts evidence orderly European architecture, Tuscan, though with a touch of the Andalusian.

To introduce his clocks, he calls on mahogany-colored, black-eyed senors, some English, German, Danish and French as well as American merchants like Dallett, shows his clock samples, leaves prices, encourages trade . . . . Oh! If only he could speak Spanish!

The itch for a new clock design so long in suspension travailing to be born quivers in his mind's eye. Will it come? Will these strange coastal mountain sights waken dormant designs lying just below the surface of his artistic mind?

Lifting his incredulous eyes up the 3,000-foot-high, nearly-perpendicular mountainside, directly over the city he distinguishes a government barracks. It adjoins the native burying ground enclosed with a wall. There, flags from look-out posts signal the approach of incoming ships sighted within a 25-mile radius of the open roadstead.

Long before the heated dawn, Elias mounts a sure-footed, unshod mule for the three or four league trek up to Caracas. He sits composedly on a native, well-stuffed rimmed saddle. It will take until noon to reach the city of Caracas . . . . If only Julia could see him now, and little Edward—they wouldn't believe their eyes!

The road presently turns due south up the mountain. The ascent is at first gradual, then steep, winding from precipice to precipice. Elias passes here and there cultivated plantations of coffee and sugarcane lying green and beautiful. He is excited by herds of wild cattle driven by llaneros in crimson and blue ponchos.

Reaching Curucuti he feels a considerable change in the atmosphere, observes the vegetation changing into verdance. Good thing he brought his overcoat from the ship's cabin—the give-away overcoat handed him by Julia at their solemn parting.

The heated, humid, acrid region of La Guayra is passed. He now meets a bland, resuscitating atmosphere. Curucuti is a stopping place for the muleteers. He sees slopes cultivated with maize, food for mules and horses. Elias dismounts from his testy, sweating beast. Stretching long legs he hardly believes he is in this wild remote Andean country so far from his quiet Connecticut home.

Over a drawbridge and into a walled esplanade, the plodding mules now enter the Salto, an old fortification. After more fatiguing travel they approach the gate at La Venta, a whitewashed inn. Here Elias finds that almost any refreshment the country affords can be had, including coffee, tea, chocolate, chicken, even ham and eggs, all served Spanish style, of course. The inn is tolerably neat and clean, but not so tidy as Julia might keep back in Bristol. Elias sups and with fascination gazes at a dramatic seaward scene.

A Majority of One 25

Now partly above clouds he is refreshed by the cool, racy atmosphere so different from the oven-like retort at La Guayra. Overlooking as from a terrace through a misty rain, he views the ocean 4,500 feet below and one part of the La Guayra roadstead. The vessels there below at anchor look like mere dinghys. He is enchanted by little green spots of cultivation and habitation clinging to the side of the mountain.

Stiffly remounting his sure-footed mule, Elias, now refreshed, wends his way round the mountain to the Cumbre, the summit. To his left he looks over a 1,000-foot, sheer drop into a valley with a few small red-roofed, white-walled cottages. (Venezuela was named from Indians building huts on stilts in lakes reminding early European explorers of Venice. Venezuela literally means "Little Venice.")

Through a tunnel-like opening at the summit, Elias views more old Spanish fortifications and lookouts on a projecting point. Here the road down to Caracas winds for nearly two miles.

Near speechless with wonder, Elias Ingraham descends the cobbled road, now passing flowering hillsides of pinks and roses, now crossing a cold stream of mountain water, now stopping for refreshment at Sanchorquiz, a tavern where the muleteers merrily imbibe of native fermented drinks—but not Puritanic Elias, the teetotaler. He is awed by mountains to the south rising to 7,000 feet above sea level.

Is all this really happening, to you, Elias Ingraham? You the unpolished Yankee, you who are looking for wood and wider clock markets in this Andean mountain valley? It is more like a dream though tempered with the realities of velvet air, the click of hooves, the Spanish jabber of muleteers, the smell of sweaty beasts, the fire of equatorial sun.

It is real, Elias, an interlude never to be forgotten, and

one never to be forgiven by your petulant Julia there in Yankeeland. Have you written her? Have you heard from her? Regular mail has just been inaugurated between La Guayra and the States. Won't you and Julia use it?

Oh drink it all in! Does the draught quench your dry longing? Allow it to waken dormant clock children in your soul. Let it bring the needed solitude for borning of new horizons before you return. Yes, drink it all in to the very last delicious dewy drop. It is a time to love.

Nobody knows how long Elias sojourned in this coastal mountain valley, where he stayed or with whom, what all he did, whether or not he wrote to or heard from his vindictive wife and whether he developed much of a clock market, or even if he was bothered by the ever-present fleas.

The only known South American city visited by Elias Ingraham was Caracas. Thus we surmise its impact on him was great. Why? Was it because of his enchantment with the majesty and grandeur of this reposeful mountain-valley scene? Was it from inspiration gained from the colorful, languid inhabitants? Did the magnificence of some Romanic-Barroco Cathedral with tremulous spires trigger the Sharp Gothic clock design? The dust of a century and a third now covers the facts. His experiences there left indelible marks in his sensitive mind. Nevertheless, from this and other inspirations, he would go on to design a thousand new clock styles to be cherished for generations to come.

Elias' long sea voyage back to New York from the Caribbean is vibrant with mind's-eye pictures collected from strange lands. He was absorbed and stimulated during these months away from the perplexities of a clock business now on the mend in Bristol. His creative mind was rested, supple, fertile, his talent ready to burst into bloom. The tranquility of the tropics, its lower key, quickens his impulse to create.

Beguiling the tedium aboard the sailing vessel plying homeward on winged winds, Elias, ever of an inventive turn of mind, itches to design a new clock, first on paper then in wood . . . . Little does he know that it will be the mantel clock talisman of the century, the clock among clocks.

Elias, scrounging below deck midst the cargo of indigo, molasses, coffee, sasparilla, india rubber, vanilla, rum, cabinet and dye woods, cotton, cognac, fruit, cocoa—finds aromatic wood from Hispaniola, Jamaica and Cuba— regular items of trade in the 1840s.

Grasping a likely two-foot-long, rough-hewn, thick, mahogany block, he clambers up a companionway onto the honed deck. His long, sensitive fingers lovingly turned the ribbon-grained mahogany over and over. With whetted knife he begins to peel, to chip, to carve away the roughness, the simple coarse geometry of that benumbed veined, reddish-brown block. Hidden beneath the rude shaggy exterior of that mahogany lies ready to emerge, to be found, phoenix-like, the most beautiful clock ever. True to his pencil drawing, representing his euphoric state of mind, the Sharp Gothic is solid evidence of reverence and majesty felt during this Caribbean tenure.

Oh, Elias! Square some there, smooth a little here, curve a mite, indent some. Cathedral-like, mold four round columns to a symmetrical, sharp peak in classic proportion. Add delicate pinnacles and tracery, emphasize vertical lines.

Little by little, hour by hour, out of a numb block, with patient, cunning hands, Elias Ingraham brings first to tropical light a new clock case destined to flower in immortality, the impeccable Sharp Gothic—and this, while it lay asleep inside a tropic West Indies block of unknowing wood.

Unlike the clock cases with carved lion paws made only for weight-driven wooden movements which Elias designed fifteen years before, this clock case was fashioned to accommodate the new, spring-wound, eight-day brass movements.

As Elias wakened this exquisite clock child from a wooden womb, the itch, that old Ingraham itch, was expiated in reverie.

Elias' search for wider markets also was a period of gestation culminating in the birth of this talisman, by far the best in point of design of any of the American clock cases of the 19th century.

"On his return to Bristol he made clock cases in accordance with this design and put them upon the market. They met with almost instant favor, and the design, under the trade name 'Sharp Gothic,' became a favorite for small shelf clocks. Had he protected the design by patent, he would have made a fortune, but since he failed to do that the design was copied by other makers and sold so extensively in this and foreign countries that it is believed to have been the 'best-seller' of any distinctively American design for clocks. Indeed, in remote parts, and particularly for export, this design still stands for reliability of performance and there is a steady demand for it . . . ." (From a 1910 newspaper article by George Dudley Seymour.)

On an incoming tide, a vessel carrying wayward Elias Ingraham home slips quietly into New York harbor. There it is berthed near The Battery and discharges its West Indian cargo.

A tall, dignified, eager, red-headed sunburned man stepped ashore, the prototype of a steeple clock lovingly tucked under his arm. A lump gathered in the throat of this talented clock designer. He was once more on American soil, going home after a year's absence. *Going home . . . going home . . . going home . . . .* The refrain rang in his ears like a Caracas church bell. A new intense light brimmed in his eyes. There was a bounce, a determination in his step.

Gathering that winter overcoat and his other belongings from the brig, he strode to the Hartford stage depot, there to step aboard the waiting vehicle.

Did there mingle with his eagerness to reunite with Julia some trepidation? After all, he had been gone 12 months from his high-strung wife whom he had asked for his winter overcoat that summer's day with nary an explanation that he was off to the tropics. How would he face her now? Would she forgive him? Time—Ingraham time—would soon tell.

He made the 100-mile bumpy trek from lower Manhattan north to Bristol. A rattling stage was something different from a smooth sailing ship, he must have mused. All the way he thrilled with the prospects of the Sharp Gothic prototype jack-knifed from the unsuspecting block of mahogany. Oh, how could he wait to show it to his dear brother, Andrew, who had come to his aid during that bankruptcy a few years back?

Partnered with Benjamin Ray, Andrew was making clocks in Elias' old clock shop. At least as early as April, 1841, Andrew had sold another of Elias' original clock designs, the Round Gothic, called the "beehive."

Surely Andrew would be excited to see this grand Sharp Gothic case. Anyone who liked clocks would love this one. Elias could scarcely wait to get into production. Why, this clock was good enough to warrant maybe even a new partnership! He'd see if Andrew and Deacon Elisha Brewster might be interested. It would be a natural. Such a firm could combine the steadfast and reliable Andrew Ingraham, the experienced, moneyed clockmaker Elisha Brewster familiar with those newish spring-driven brass clock movements, and Elias' own unmatched design talent and skill in joinery. What a trinity!

He'd tell them about wider clock markets abroad—in South and Central America, the West Indies, Europe, even Asia. They could name the new company Brewster and Ingrahams. They might have to take in coffee or mahogany in exchange for their clocks, but who wasn't already accustomed to such barter . . . ? Meanwhile, he could work for Ray and Ingraham and perfect his treasured steeple clock.

That virginal block of wood now whittled into a graceful clock prototype indeed merited his high hopes. For the first Sharp Gothic clocks bearing the name Brewster and Ingrahams met with almost instant success, becoming a favorite among small shelf clocks.

Midst the scramble of forming the new company, the need for working drawings and details for many new Ingraham designed clocks, demands of tooling, fabricating and assembling these clocks in mass production, marketing through dealers new and old, at home and abroad—midst all these demands, sadly, Elias failed to patent his beautiful steeple clock child. Pirates included competitors like Chauncey Jerome and a score more. Hundreds of thousands were thus marketed around the world with and without the Ingraham moniker.

The Sharp Gothic clock and a large number of Elias' other designs eventually made for him what was considered a fortune in his day. But for now, the need was to bail him out of debt even though it took years.

A full quarter century after the death of Elias Ingraham—more than sixty years after the birth of the Sharp Gothic—it still stood reliable in performance, unmatched in its own original grace, having a steady demand in remote parts around the world.

As tasteful as was the Sharp Gothic, it was not elegant enough to mollify an irate Julia Ingraham left to fend for herself for the year. Among her apparently inherited characteristics from the Sparks family was a sharp tongue and she had good reason to use it on her deviate husband. And use it she did!

Solid menfolk there in New England just didn't run off like that! When they did, they really heard about it. Errant Elias was no exception. It all bit into Julia's soul. She never forgave him, rehearsed the story as long as she lived, never telling it without a recurrence of her old resentment.

Who could blame her? Was her indignation not righteous? How would any spouse appreciate being left alone while her mate embarks on a "wild gothic chase" to Caracas?

Even so, and notwithstanding the Sharp Gothic vs. a sharp tongue, on September 3, 1843, Julia Ingraham by "profession of faith," joined the Bristol, Connecticut, Congregational Church quite soon after Elias' return . . . . Did her conscience bother her?

The only fanciful act of any consequence, if indeed seeking wider clock markets could be deemed wanton, was Elias' year-long absence from Julia without notice. However, his itch to travel recurred, his yen to see distant places and new horizons occasionally hounded him thereafter. Even so, subsequent affairs compelled disciplines less noticeable than in those early roaring forties.

Elias' yearning to travel and his later economic ability to do so transmitted itself down through the Ingraham line for generations to come. They all still love to travel and do so with abandon.

There is much more to tell of the early years before Caracas about this indomitable genius who designed hundreds of styles of 19th century American shelf clocks and sold them around the world by the hundreds of thousands, as the following chapters reveal.

2

Blossoms on the Family Tree

1133-1804

Our ancestors are very good kind of folks; but they are the last people I should choose to have a visiting acquaintance with.
—Richard Grinsley Sheridan

Great men are both the products and the shapers of their times. Talent without opportunity may be wasted. Opportunity without talent can be wasteful.

Elias Ingraham was the product of a Puritanical New England heritage, a shaper of 19th century Yankee Americana. His talent was wedded to the opportunity of a young nation's hunger for more than bare necessities. Among 19th century American clock designers he was without a peer. In his lifetime he neither wasted his talent nor lacked struggle and opportunity as he maintained a tender foresight which considered generations still to come.

The ancestral line of Connecticut-born Elias Ingraham runs deep into antiquity. His mother, Eunice Carrier, was descended from a Thomas Carrier. In 1649, accord-

Blossoms on the Family Tree 33

ing to tradition, Thomas was the bodyguard for, or the executioner of, Charles I of England. The high court of justice convicted Charles I of treason and beheaded him. Thomas Carrier, though but twenty or twenty-one, may have wielded the fatal axe.

Carrier, alias Morgan, afterward fled to America. In 1664 he married Martha Allen of Welsh ancestry whom the courts of Salem, Massachusetts later executed on the gallows for witchcraft.

"He was one hundred and nine years old . . . not grey or bald, walked erect, and shortly before his death walked six miles," a *New England Weekly Journal* article said of Thomas Carrier.

The terror of witchcraft reached its apex in Salem towards the end of the seventeenth century. Elias Ingraham's maternal ancestor, Martha Allen Carrier, was entangled in that barbarity.

In Salem, Harvard educated, thirty-year-old Cotton Mather, a Congregational minister, roused the village against the purported evil work of witches. As a result of his religious perversity, nineteen innocents were put to death in 1692. These were the last executions for witchcraft in the American Colonies.

At least two sons and a daughter were with Martha Carrier: Richard, Andrew and Sarah. The sons refused to confess anything while they were tied neck and heels with blood gushing from their noses. Martha Carrier was hanged by recorded forced testimony of seven-year-old Sarah.

Martha was linked with a witch named Aunt Toothaker. At her own hearing Martha talked back to the court and showed unusual spirit. Though a victim of malicious gossip, Martha Allen Carrier was condemned and hanged ignominiously. It is unknown why Thomas was not in

Salem to defend and support his wife in her cruel extremity.

Pricked by its conscience seventeen years later, a Massachusetts court paid to the Carrier family heirs the sum of seven pounds six shillings in token restitution.

Soon after Martha's death, the peppery Thomas Carrier and two sons removed to the more benign atmosphere of Connecticut, first to Colchester, thence to Marlborough, pioneering its settlement by 1698. Thomas and Martha Carrier's great-great-granddaughter, Eunice Carrier Ingraham, delivered her first born son on October 1, 1805 in the self-same Marlborough. This boy inherited from his maternal ancestors the endurance of Thomas Carrier, the spirit of Martha Carrier and the courage of them both. He was Elias Ingraham.

Eunice Carrier of Marlborough, born March 17, 1774, was married in 1803 to Joseph Ingraham III, who was born four days after the signing of the Declaration of Independence.

Elias' paternal ancestors, though colonial pioneers, were less colorful than the Carriers. The Ingrahams in America originated in the colonies through Richard Ingraham six generations before Elias. In 1639 Richard came from England to Marblehead, removing later to Rehoboth, Massachusetts. He emigrated during the religious and political unrest of the Charles I reign, the same unrest which ten years later culminated in the king's beheading, according to tradition, by Thomas Carrier. Thus it was that both maternal and paternal ancestors of Elias Ingraham reached America within a few decades of each other from the same Mother England, leaving a country embroiled in political turmoil.

Joseph Ingraham II, grandfather of Elias, served in the militia company of Captain Amos Jones in the late summer of 1777. Many other Ingrahams were Royalists

Blossoms on the Family Tree 35

and fled to Canada during the American Revolution. The revolt was not altogether popular. Of the colonials, one-third were in favor, a third were opposed, and the other third didn't care.

The census of 1790 records Joseph Ingraham II, in New London County, as head of a family with one white female, Elias' grandmother. Strangely, their teenaged son, Joseph III, was not listed. Perhaps at fourteen he was apprenticed or for other reasons was absent from his parents' home or their thoughts.

Two hundred pound, six-foot tall George Washington took the oath of office in New York City as first president in 1789. The agricultural nation assumed its own reins in a fledgling government. Of the four million inhabitants of the young nation, 700,000 were slaves, most of whom labored on the large southern plantations. The dignified Washington died in 1799, six years prior to Elias Ingraham's birth.

John Adams succeeded Washington to the presidency, serving until 1801. Adams was a learned, thoughtful, political philosopher and lawyer. He prophetically asserted, "People and Nations are forged in the fires of adversity." Elias Ingraham would one day know what those words meant. Harvard educated, diplomatic, moderate Adams kept the country out of impending war with Napoleonic France. He and Jefferson died on the fiftieth anniversary of the Declaration of Independence in 1826. That year Elias Ingraham served his last year as an apprentice cabinet maker.

In restless France, thirty-year-old Napoleon, the "Little Corporal" from Corsica, came to power the same year as Washington's death. Accounts of his military exploits rumbled over half the globe until Elias was ten years old.

Jedidiah Morse, D.D., in 1800 saw the fledgling nation arising fast to maturity with prospects of vigorous and prosperous national manhood. Agriculture was the spring of commerce and the parent of manufacturing.

Morse wrote of religion of this period "that it is left to be supported by its own evidence, by the lives of its professors, and the almighty care of its office, all being left at liberty to choose their own religion." Elias Ingraham followed a Puritanical tradition and was himself an earnest and pious churchman all his life.

The distribution of wealth in Connecticut was more equal than elsewhere with a minimum of excess or want of wealth. New England was the nursery of men who were the transplants into other parts of the young nation, albeit Elias lived and worked within forty miles of his birthplace.

Morse estimated that the Indian population at this time was two and a half million in all of North America. By 1800 Connecticut's population numbered fewer than 250,000 citizens, including 4,000 slaves.

The Ingrahams, like most New Englanders, stemmed from English descent, lived on their own farms, and enjoyed comfortable though plain living. Most were Congregationalists as were the Ingrahams. Connecticut maintained political stability, allowing opportunity for individual enterprise and initiative as embodied in the omniactive Yankee Peddler. Elias Ingraham was not much of a peddler but he certainly was a Yankee. The bulk of Connecticut inhabitants were industrious, temperate, independent, sagacious, quietly humorous husbandmen, a pattern of humanity recognizable in the sturdy Ingraham lineage.

Morse quaintly described the farmer, "marrying young, strong and healthful from cultivating his farm where he toils cheerfully through the day with gladsome heart and at night devoutly thanks his bounteous God for his blessings daily, retires to rest and his sleep is sweet."

Blossoms on the Family Tree

Farmers' lives were disciplined by the rigors of pioneer life and Puritanical faith, disciplines that molded and shaped the character of Elias Ingraham and promoted his success.

Strict adherence to Sabbath keeping was an Ingraham heritage. Behavior such as the rules below prescribe what was expected:

"No one shall run on the Sabbath Day, or walk in his garden, except reverently to and from meeting.

"No woman shall kiss her child on the Sabbath or fasting day.

"No one shall travel, cook victuals, make beds, sweep houses, cut hair, or shave on the Sabbath Day.

"Every male shall have his hair cut round according to a cap.

"No gospel minister shall join people in marriage. The magistrate may join them, as he may do it with less scandal to Christ's Church.

"A man who strikes his wife shall be fined ten dollars.

"A woman who strikes her husband shall be punished as the law directs.

"Whoever publishes a lie to the prejudice of his neighbor shall sit in the stocks, or be whipped fifteen stripes.

"When parents refuse their children convenient marriages, the magistrate shall decide the point.

"No one shall read common prayer, keep Christmas or Saint days, make minced pies, dance, play cards, or play on any instrument of music except the drum, trumpet, and Jew's harp.

"No one shall be a freeman or have a vote, unless he is converted and a member of one of the churches allowed in the dominion."

(From the *General History of Connecticut* by Rev. Samuel Peters)

Such deportment was severe but severe were the times. Not indulgence but survival lay just below the surface. Conservative, deeply religious Yankees, like the Ingrahams and Carriers, had the moral fiber and the mental sinew that characterized the New England stock of the eighteenth century.

In 1805 Spain still held California, having a Spanish population of hardly 3,000 souls, mostly mixed breeds. Pueblo de Los Angeles had but a hundred families. To rural New Englanders like Joseph and Eunice Ingraham, California was a distant unknown wilderness, though their son, Elias, would journey there in 1873.

With its granite hills and matching men, Connecticut had a flare for inventive firsts. More patents have been granted to Connecticut inventors than to those of any other state in proportion to population. Many patents would be issued to Elias for his original clock case designs although his famous Sharp Gothic case would remain unpatented and widely copied.

Within this framework of Yankee New England Elias was born of Joseph III and Eunice Ingraham. Having talent, with opportunity united to ambition, this son was destined to be a product and shaper of his time. He was born into that wondrous season when the green fruit of the nation's young tree ripened into hardy though not always sweet fruitage.

3

Up from the Sod

1805-1820

Get thy spindle and thy distaff ready, and God will send the flax.
—New England Folklore

A four-stringed violin vibrating a melody composed for a multi-stringed piano can hardly reproduce the original score. But the variations may be more dissimilar if a century and a half intervenes between the playing of the original unrecorded melody and the repetition.

The chronicler of Elias Ingraham must use empathy to reconstruct Elias' life. Precious little data exists between the time of his birth in 1805 and the completion of his apprenticeship in 1827.

At the age of four, Elias' father was baptized in the faith on October 14, 1780. Joseph Ingraham Jr. and his wife were received into membership May 6, 1827, the very month their elder son, Elias, began his career as a clock designer in Bristol, Connecticut. In 1831 Elias Ingraham's brother, Andrew, and their grandparents joined as members of the Marlborough Congregational Church.

The dawn of the nineteenth century presaged an era

during which greater changes would occur than in the twenty centuries preceding. The seventeen-state nation of 1805 began a metamorphosis from an agricultural to an industrial economy. Every decade of this century added discoveries altering the outlook and life of mankind.

Into this severe life and land Elias Ingraham was born on an October Indian summer day. Work, work, work was the means and measure of survival. The fiber and sinew within Elias were forged in this rural crucible beginning in the cradle.

The naming of children, even villages, in New England was often sourced in the Bible. Five of the first seven Ingraham generations in America bore scriptural first names: Joseph I, Nathaniel, Joseph II, Joseph Jr., and then Elias (the Greek for Elijah meaning "Jehovah is my God"), and Andrew, his younger brother.

When Elias Ingraham's parents named him for the prophet, Elijah, did they divine the conjunction that their son would have with that great Bible character? Both were dynamic, leaders; both shaped history and dominated their times and thought. Elijah was fleet of foot. So was Elias (his maternal ancestor, Thomas Carrier, ran fast even when 108 years old). Both were robust, having rugged constitutions. Elijah resisted famine. So did Elias who eventually suffered through bankruptcy and fire. Both were courageous, God-fearing, resolute and resilient. The authority of the still, small voice that Elijah heeded at Mount Horeb, Elias heard as an ascending, developing profile of a thousand clock designs. Emerging from a simple agrarian state into a complex form of society, they both made their mark. To Elijah, Israel was the laboratory; to Elias, it was Bristol.

Elias and Andrew were born of heavenly-minded par-

Up from the Sod 41

ents. These boys inherited characteristics formed in rural simplicity by sturdy and frugal progenitors. The Bible was their family friend and food from earliest childhood. Throughout their lives scriptural teachings outlined their ambitions, characterized their motives, and directed their footsteps. Prudent Joseph and Eunice Ingraham, who were married on December 28, 1803, by John Isom of Colchester, Connecticut, reared their offspring in sober, Christian piety, an atmosphere that sustained and dominated long and eventful lives.

Joseph Ingraham Jr., like other contemporary Marlborough dirt farmers, rose with the light and went to bed with the dark. He wore chiefly the things that his own labor and that of Eunice produced. His own legs or the legs of horses or oxen were his transportation. His farmhouse had no running water, no inside plumbing, no furnace, no coal stove, no electrical light, not even matches. The fire in the fireplace was ash-banked at night to last until morning.

Epaphroditus Peck, writing in *Four Half Centuries in Bristol,* recalls a story by one of his ancestors . . .

> . . . who said that at night his mother used to blow the back log into a lively flame, and then cover it carefully with ashes, hoping that the fire would last through the night. But sometimes it would fail, and in the morning the log would be cold. Then she would go outdoors, and look around the neighborhood to see if smoke was coming out of any of the chimneys. If she saw the welcome sign of a fire, she would send a child with a pail to 'borrow a fire.' The obliging neighbor would blow up an ember, pack it in ashes, and tell the child to run home with the precious brand, so that his mother could start a fire from it.

We can imagine Mother Eunice Ingraham standing outside the kitchen door hopefully looking for smoke from a neighbor's chimney and sending little Elias with a pail to "borrow a fire."

Women at forty often died from hardships, although Elias' mother lived to be sixty-seven. His father died at eighty-two. Gravestones indicated a high infant mortality, but the Ingraham boys both survived with great longevity.

Babies and grownups died of accidents no longer common: falling into the fire, or into a pot of boiling water, falling off a roof into a water wheel, falling through ice, or having a buggy turn over and pinning a young driver in the stream. No such calamities befell the little Ingraham brothers though their fibre was otherwise tried and tested throughout their lives.

Built largely with the help of neighbors, the Ingraham house and barn, like others of the period, were made of rough timber cut from the land. Split rail or stone fences surrounded meadows of "neat cattle," or lesser livestock. The scant, flat acres produced corn and wheat, rye and oats. Barnyards and meadows held noisy poultry, oxen, horses, sheep and swine. The indispensable, versatile beast of burden, the ox, produced meat, leather and even milk.

Besides the fireplace, candles or whale oil lamps provided artificial light. The Ingraham farmhouse contained only the bare necessities. Eunice cooked on the open fireplace hearth, which was the only heat in the bitter winters. Corn was the mainstay of food in the form of "journey cake," or "johnny cake." Meat and fish were salted and smoked for later use.

Before the flickering fire flame, visualize the Ingraham four at supper: bearded Joseph at the head of the table, bland Eunice opposite, and sons Elias and Andrew peering at each other across the table filled with simple but plentiful provender. Elias was destined for industrial fame and fortune. Andrew, more agrarian and less talented, nevertheless shared in and contributed to his brother's success.

Warming pans of hot embers were put under bed covers at night in the harsh winters. Farmers and their families spent winters and rainy days mostly inside engaged in homespun craftsmanship or repairs to equipment and tools. Elias thereby early learned to be handy and resourceful, patient and persistent.

For generations, Ingrahams whimsically declared, "We have two seasons, winter and the Fourth of July"; and "The New England climate consists of nine months winter and three months late in the Fall."

The welcome spring found the Ingrahams in the plodderies of plowing, planting and plucking. They filled hot, humid days and summer nights with toil, tilling, tending and tanning. Harvests were gleaned in the mellowness of autumn and stored, stocked, stowed, salted, seasoned and spiced against winter's sterility. Stoical, indifferent, pink-cheeked Yankee husbandmen like Joseph Ingraham, Jr., accepted the extremities of terrain and climate as routine and taught their children accordingly.

The Ingrahams' antecedents owned and operated grist mills and saw mills. Elias was early acquainted not only with farming but with water-power-driven machinery. He coaxed fortune and fame from clocks made from water-powered contrivances, while Andrew in later life sold water wheels, by then nearly out of fashion.

Far away in the hills of frontier Kentucky, Tom Lincoln and Nancy Hanks were married in June 1806 at Elizabethtown. The village, a century and a half later, would include a prosperous factory bearing the name of an Ingraham child who now lay taciturn in his distant

Connecticut crib, an eight-month-old infant named Elias Ingraham.

When Elias was four years old, a child named Abraham was born to Tom and Nancy Lincoln—a son whom they named also for a Biblical patriarch, a baby destined to fill a desperate need in the nation's life-and-death struggle in the slavery issue.

As Elias was learning to walk, the young nation like a giant magnet again drew to its shores foreigners from the turbulent European continent. The voyage to America took six to twelve hard weeks. Those who landed safely had their courage and stamina further tried. Many such immigrants later worked for Elias in his clock factories.

In 1808, when Elias was three, gloom settled over the nation, including Marlborough. The problems of getting the young country started were heavy and frequent. Relations with antagonized Mother England were bad, and growing worse. President Jefferson and Congress instituted an embargo on our ships sailing abroad. Business was ruined, especially in the more industrial New England. Bankruptcy was prevalent.

Down in Louisiana, Jean Lafitte smuggled African slaves into the south, selling males at $400, females at $325 and boys at $200 in violation of the federal law just enacted prohibiting slave trade.

In 1809 predatory Spain nominally controlled California, Florida, Mexico and most of South America.

Sailing ships plied the oceans of the world, ships dependent upon the vagaries of wind and tide.

The era in America was one of broad family unity. During this God-fearing, family-loving period, the nation morally bloomed and spiritually blossomed through the character and lives of sturdy New Englanders like the Ingrahams.

Up from the Sod

The gloom of New England deepened when war was again declared against mighty England on June 18, 1812. Elias was nearly seven years old. Flags hung at half-mast. Bells tolled plaintively against the war. Though woefully unprepared, the United States successfully prosecuted the War of 1812 because England had her hands full with Napoleon. Had Elias listened, he could have heard the roar of cannon like distant thunder in a battle on the Connecticut River between ships of the two antagonists.

At the end of the unpopular war with England an era of wakening industrial, cultural and social thought followed the creative political science periods of the Revolution. Elias Ingraham rose on this exciting wave and contributed to its momentum. The age-old cup of toil of man and animal cracked. The human, the animal, wind, falling water and tide as sources of power and transportation were replaced by machines both stationary and mobile. Elias beheld this adjustment and contributed to it.

The first roads were Indian paths later widened and smoothed into turnpikes. Some were known as corduroy roads made of logs laid across the road bed, helping to keep horses and oxen out of mud but making travel rough. The word "travel" comes from the root meaning travail, and so it was. Improved transportation modes were dawning: railroads, canals, clipper ships, turnpikes and steamboats. Virgin lands were opening in the West, increasing the markets for the burgeoning factories of the East.

Using "fast" sailing ships between New York and Liverpool, the Black Ball Line initiated a regular transatlantic service in 1816. The same year sixteen thousand wagons headed west on one turnpike alone in Pennsylvania. Men hungered for new land, new ideas and new opportunities. It was said of those who headed west, "The cowards never started and the weak ones died by the way." Elias sought and found his fortune within one day's journey of his birthplace and supplied clocks to pioneers and their families at home, in the West and around the world.

The few letters extant in Elias' and Andrew's handwriting are delightful for their misspelling. Their formal schooling was of short duration. Elias and Andrew certainly were at recess during the spelling exercises.

In the first quarter of the nineteenth century, Marlborough had its one-room school situated opposite the meeting house. All grades were held in the same classroom. The older children sat at the rear. Recalcitrant students were banished to woodroom or attic for punishment or whacked with an omnipresent ruler in the hands of the omnipotent schoolmaster.

School was kept during but four of the winter months. The Ingraham boys at nine or ten labored on the farms in spring, summer, and fall. At fourteen, they did the work of men. The education of girls was not considered important and Elias' future wife, Julia, of nearby Glastonbury, was favored with little schooling. The schools taught reading, writing, geography, grammar, arithmetic, spelling and the Bible. Elias ciphered with a slate pencil sharpened by a pocket knife, or quills from grey goose wings. Blackboards were unthought-of until long after. Teachers were often under twenty, boarded by the gentry. Their pay for teaching was five or ten dollars a month for women, ten to twenty a month for men, plus board. Neither Elias nor Andrew attended high school since none existed in Marlborough until later. Their higher education came from the school of hard knocks and they graduated with honors.

4

At the Master's Bench

1821-1826

No man is born into the world whose work is not born with him.
　　　　　—Irving Stone
　　　　　　The Agony and the Ecstasy

There is manhood in him who tries though he fail. Pity him who loses by default, who fails without trying, for the way to win may involve doubling the failures.

Thankfully Elias Ingraham did not succumb to complacency, nor was he stunted by mediocrity. Life's external demands, coupled with an inner drive, wakened exceptionality. His accomplishments were nine parts sweat to one part intuitive endowment. Like a plucky chick from the inside out he pecked open his shell, like the chick he was strengthened in the process and stepped out of middling confinement.

See him now, blue-green-eyed, red-headed Elias Ingraham, embracing his tearful mother, bidding farewell to his ruddy, bearded father, saying good-bye to fourteen-year-old admiring Andrew. The era of precious childhood was now gone for Elias. Manhood, almost premature, had suddenly overtaken him. No longer would he

47

depend on home, hearth and hand of those dear parents. The contract bound him to a master in Glastonbury for a five-year apprenticeship to learn cabinetry.

It is sad that generations to come will never know the name of the master cabinetmaker to whom Elias was bound in Glastonbury. Would that his name were known so that credit honorably due might be given. Those years of Elias' apprenticeship formed lasting qualities of the ensemble of manhood called Elias Ingraham. Doubtless his master was responsible for wakening, fashioning and directing the young man's innate talent.

Dr. Lee J. Whittles of Glastonbury has speculated who Elias' master might have been. He knows the name of no cabinetmaker in Glastonbury in the 1820's. Dr. Whittles conjectures that Elias' first interest as a woodworker could have been from a gunsmith of Glastonbury named Buell, who fashioned wooden gun butts. The Buell shop was but two miles from Marlborough, within Elias' easy walking distance in most any kind of weather. However, it is clear that Elias' training in joinery was not limited to gun butts.

Apprentice training grew from craft guilds in European medieval times. Promising lads were instructed in the trade and maintained in return for their services. At first Elias ran errands, made fires, cleaned the shop, and acted as servant to his master. Picking up knowledge of the mechanical work, he soon took his place at the bench assisting with simpler parts of the productive work. Eventually he became sufficiently skilled to handle any of the work in the shop, finally becoming a journeyman.

View the teen-aged apprentice there in the fragrant cabinet shop. Observe his master—seasoned, serious, solicitous.

See the bins of boards of various woods waiting to be turned or joined: the tawny pliable pine; the honey-

At the Master's Bench

colored, hard, dense, maple; the tough, open-grained oak; the structural fir; the tightgrained, dense birch; the regal laurel; the off-white speckled irregular-grained beech; the dense-grained, reddish cherry; the nearly black, close-grained, rich walnut; the durable chestnut so useful to the farmer; the tough elm; the aromatic cedar; the variegated, exotic rosewood; and the ribbon-grained, pinkish-brown mahogany.

Hear his master quietly but firmly teaching him how to work with wood, not to fight it but to love it, to feel its character and capacity. Witness him instructing Elias, the novice, to see the natural forms within the wood, never to grow angry or unsympathetic towards it. He shows Elias how wood works with the craftsman, reveals itself, is seen and sawn and shaped and sized correctly. Each wood, each board has its own character and you must understand it. Then it will give of itself to your love and skill.

Observe Elias now at his bench. Note well the aptness with which he handles the gauge, square, chalkline, adze, drawknife, plane, bit, keyhole saw, chisel, gimlet, hammer and lathe. Observe the growing dexterity as he marks, measures, saws, files, bores, miters, nails, screws, glues, and assembles the wood into final form. Note Elias' modest pride as his master examines with approval the turning, mortising and tenoning, the coping and mitering, the drilling and sanding, the splaying, splicing, building and finishing. He is learning to make cabinets, chairs, coffins, tables, cupboards, bedsteads, drawers, chests, looking glass frames, benches, desks.

See standing in the corner near a tool chest that handsome classic tall cherry clock case—the first fashioned, fabricated and finished by this eager and willing lad. Little does he suspect that his life work lies ahead hidden in millions of clockcases.

Now that his young charge is showing such an adeptness at fabricating the master sets young Elias at the drawing board. There he finds more delicate tools of design: the compass, scale, square, divider, pencil, eraser, drawing paper. You can't always make out of a board what can be drawn on paper with a pencil. Elias is finding the horizontalism of plane geometry, the revealment of solid geometry, the relevance of accuracy to perfection, the necessity to make aesthetics practical, the golden mean of proportion. All are indispensable aspects of the whole.

While training as a joiner, Elias was exposed to manuals of design and furniture making. A revival of Gothic architecture was entering the American cultural scene. This revival twenty years later materialized in Elias Ingraham's classical clock cases of Gothic design, which would rule clock case styling for half a century.

On Sunday, his only day off, true to his Puritanic heritage, Elias attended church services at the Glastonbury meeting house. The church was established in 1693. Begun in 1735, the sanctuary was typical of the period, forty feet wide, fifty-six feet long, and thirty-five feet high between the joists. The pulpit was high, overhung by a huge sounding board. The pews were high-backed, latticed. Restless children peeked at each other, wearied by the length and contents of the sermons.

Toward the end of Elias' apprenticeship, the church had as its temporary preacher, from January 1826 to June 1827, the Rev. Samuel Griswold, who brought about a revival in the church, converting nearly a hundred members. Elias Ingraham was among these converts.

It is Sunday, June 18, 1826, in Glastonbury. The meeting house is filled. The Rev. Mr. Griswold is in the pulpit on the west side, having ascended the steps. The pews closest to the pulpit are filled with village dignitaries.

At the Master's Bench

The nether sit behind them and in the galleries flanking the back of the unadorned sanctuary. Humble black servants sit in somewhat raised seats at the minister's right in the rear southeast corner.

See there those two young men, side by side, scrubbed, pressed, combed, clean-shaven, in their Sunday-go-to-meetin' best. Already with noble bearing, Elias has nearly completed his indenture and is now a senior apprentice. His friend George Warren, five years older, is already a fullfledged journeyman. This very day they are both baptized in the faith and listed on the church roll.

Meanwhile Elias has been sparkin' some. Dour, eighteen-year-old Julia Sparks sits nearby with her parents, Nathan and Lucinda Hale Sparks. She has her acquisitive eye on the leonine red-haired, blue-green-eyed, handsome Elias Ingraham. The Sparks parents already suspect that at no distant date a wedding will transpire uniting Julia, their fourth of eight children, and this promising, modest Elias Ingraham. They could not know that another of their daughters would become the third and last wife of Andrew Ingraham half a century later.

The fifth and last year of Elias' apprenticeship was spent with Daniel Dewey of Hartford just across the recently built covered wooden bridge over the Connecticut River. Elias completed four years with his Glastonbury master. Purchasing his fifth year, he trudged the six miles to the Dewey shop, and there, really started his career.

Why did Elias purchase his fifth year of apprenticeship and with what? Why was he released? No one knows. Perhaps the master could not maintain him, or perhaps Elias had learned in four years what others learned in five or more. He was just that able, willing, and talented.

Elias spent his fifth year working as a journeyman in

the cabinet shop of Daniel Dewey. According to the 1825 Hartford City Directory, Daniel Dewey had a cabinet and chair warehouse. Fourteen years earlier, the American Mercury had the following advertisement:

> Cabinet Furniture—The subscribers have commenced the cabinet making business under the firm name of Gillett and Dewey at the shop lately occupied by Samuel Bechwith, a few yards south of the brick Meeting House where may be had a variety of sideboards, secretaries, bureaus, tables, sofas, bedsteads, etc., made in the best manner and will be sold on reasonable terms. B. C. Gillett, D. Dewey, May 27, 1812, Hartford.

That year in Hartford broadened Elias' horizons, advanced his skills in art and business, and developed his awareness of the growing clockwork in nearby Bristol. Opportunity then knocked at his door which opened simultaneously both from within and from without.

In May of 1827 Alonzo Hinman, an uncle and business associate of George Mitchell of Bristol, recognized the talent and promise of Elias' work in the Dewey shop. Hinman asked Elias to come to Bristol to design a clock to compete with the Chauncey Jerome clock. Elias accepted.

Destiny now beckoned Elias to his lifework and home. Reminiscent of the prophet Samuel, who sat not down until the shepherd David was brought to him for anointing, so fortune restlessly waited in Bristol twenty-eight centuries later for another, if lesser, lad of ability. The gestation period was over. A distinguished career was a-bornin'.

Elias' hand tools were regularly swung over his shoulders. Tools of another kind, even more important than those on his strong back, lay alive in his mind and spirit, mental tools keen and sharp, willing and ready. His

At the Master's Bench

talents were now trained, his opportunity waited, beckoned. The tools of hand and heart combined into a remarkable career to last for fifty-eight years and into a company to last for generations still to come.

His path back to Bristol lay past West Society, through the modest hills of the Talcott range, hard by the village of Farmington and the big bend area, past Rattlesnake Mountain, beyond the Farmington River, across the Scott's Swamp area, through Forestville, across the North Fork of the Pequabuck, and thence to beckoning, beloved Bristol.

Years later Elias wrote, "I had served five years' apprenticeship for the cabinet business. I had made a contract with George Mitchell to work on clock cases one year for one dollar twenty-five cents per day and twelve hours for a day's work."

The fifty-three-year-old Mitchell needed a new clockcase to gain advantage over the ambitious thirty-four-year-old Chauncey Jerome. Elias Ingraham, though but twenty-one, was just the man to design and make such a clock case. And he did! His career to last for generations now began in earnest.

5

The City that Could

1827

*These were men of pith and thew,
Whom the city never called;
Scarce could read or hold a quill,
Built the barn, the forge, the mill.*
—Edmund Blunden

One can better appreciate the life of Elias Ingraham if he draws back the dusty curtains from the Connecticut community of Bristol to observe its origin, settlement, struggles and resources.

The story of a village, like that of an individual, is one of overcoming. It is also the story of the simultaneous use of natural and human resources. The tale of Bristol, like that of Elias Ingraham, is an account of the development of American backbone. Heritages lie in the disciplines, struggles, hardships, failures and victories of ancestors.

Named "noisy" by the Tunxis Indians, the mellifluous Pequabuck River creamed down a rocky channel. The area had been an Indian hunting ground for centuries. A conifer forest covered the rocky hills abounding with deer, bear, squirrel, rabbit, wild turkey, wolf, panther and wild cat.

The City that Could 55

Every spring migrations of swarming shad and salmon from the ocean ascended rivers and brooks. The Tunxis Indians, primarily fish eaters, depended upon the migrating salmon and shad for their principal diet.

Friendly relations between whites and the Tunxis Indians existed from the first coming of the white man in the seventeenth century. The Tunxis were peaceful, afraid of the Mohawks who sometimes ravaged their villages near the Connecticut River's big bend. They welcomed the early whites as confederates in the defense against the predatory Mohawks.

The future site of the town of Bristol was hilly, rocky, wooded and well watered. In the central part was a rise later called Federal Hill, where there were rock outcroppings left from the glacial period; to the northwest lay another rise later called Chippins Hill, a name derived from an Indian word. Southward ran a third rise known as South Mountain.

Rock underlay Federal Hill which one day would become a triangular 300 by 600 foot village green. To the north side a meeting house would rise.

East of the future village of Bristol lay an area later called Forestville—flat, heavily wooded, where the Pequabuck wound through the valley towards the Farmington River.

The first white settlers at Hartford in the mid 1630s, like the Indians, largely subsisted on the wild life of the forests and stream. Pushing westward from Hartford, early white hunters found the rich lands cultivated by the Tunxis near Farmington and discovered the abundance of game in the forests beyond.

The first name for the section now known as Bristol was "Pole-land." It was named for the ample hoop poles found in the forests. From these woods, coopers took oak and hickory for hoops and staves to be used in barrels, casks, tubs, buckets, butter churns, and wooden pipes.

The first white settlers in Pole-land were Daniel Brownson in 1727 and Ebenezer Barnes and Nehemiah Manross in 1728. Exactly one hundred years intervened between Bristol's first settler and Elias Ingraham's arrival.

Some of the lumber from Ebenezer Barnes' original house is incorporated into the Barnes wing of the American Clock and Watch Museum now in Bristol.

In 1735 the village, then called New Cambridge, comprised less than a dozen houses.

After traveling the nine miles to the Farmington meeting house for fourteen years in summer and winter, twenty families, led by Ebenezer Barnes, petitioned for local winter preaching privileges. The establishment of a Winter Society followed in 1742, becoming Bristol's own first organization of the Congregational Church. Thus the meeting house of Farmington begat the Society of Bristol. Elias and Andrew Ingraham, a century later, were members of that church.

In 1748 the congregation first occupied the new meeting house. This unpainted, steepled meeting house (so called rather than a church by liturgical dissenters) was forty feet by thirty feet, a plain building with galleries and traditional high pulpit.

Reminiscent of the Glastonbury meeting house, the gentry held pews closest to the pulpit. The plebeian sat toward the rear. Boys at sixteen and girls at fourteen were finally admitted to these pews.

Disestablishment between church and state resulted in a Sunday school in 1818.

Between the morning and afternoon services the faithful warmed or rested in the row of "sabba'-day houses" near the stocks and whipping posts. At this very spot in

The City that Could 57

1828, Constable Newman Peck administered the last legal whipping in Connecticut. Did Elias witness that brutality? Did Julia, his bride of one year?

George Hull has written of a minister's status of that period:

> In every way he was the leader of the community, always its best and, in most instances the only, educated man. When he came within sight of the church the bell was tolled; when he entered, everyone rose and saluted; and when he preached from the high colonial pulpit, he seemed the very oracle of God. On every important matter, his advice was sought.

As a youth, Elias was taught this Westminster Catechism:

> That I must abstain on the Sabbath from all kinds of business done for gain or livelihood, which, by prudent management, might have been done previously, or may be left undone till after the Sabbath; that I must abstain from the reading of newspapers and books that are not religious; from studying the arts and sciences; from writing letters upon worldly topics and interests; from keeping up accounts and posting books; from unnecessary travelling; from walking and riding for pleasure; from conversing about general news of the time, trade, politics, etc.; from feasting and visiting of friends and neighbors, from unnecessary preparation of food and other manual labors.
>
> (From *The First Congregational Church of Bristol*, p. 31)

In 1741 Joseph Plumb built the first gristmill on the Pequabuck. Joseph Atkins constructed the first saw mill a year or two later. A dam was built soon after.

Roads were unbelievably bad, often merely quagmires

over Indian trails. Passage was laborious, often impossible. Peddlers used lightly loaded carts hard even for one horse to haul, making perhaps ten miles per day. The Midland Turnpike came through Bristol in 1804, presaging the transition from an agricultural to an industrial community.

Wolves plagued the homesteaders, though the beasts were suspicious of the zig-zag rail fences that surrounded barnyards and meadows. Settlers cleared their homesteads, planted corn, flax, hay crops, vegetable gardens, orchards and grain. Homes were of rough sawn clapboard, roofs of hand split shingles. Every house had a fireplace and chimney. Life was simple, hard, often dangerous.

Blacksmiths made nearly all the tools for the farm tinker shops. These shops fathered manufacturies launched by inventive Yankees like Elias Ingraham who shaped industrial Connecticut for generations to come.

Bears still roamed the forests by 1750. Deer were abundant well through the lifetime of Elias Ingraham.

The first tannery was built and operated by Jabez Roberts. Though the tanners' products were indispensable, the process involved objectionable smells. Tanners were therefore not exactly popular. Roberts' tanning materials were secured from the nearby forests, hemlock bark for the tanning of sole leather, oak bark for the uppers, and sumac for the linings and soft leathers.

Most inhabitants of New Cambridge farmed for the entire eighteenth century and for one-third of the nineteenth. Shop work was done by thrifty and clever people to pick up extra money on rainy days or during the winter. Tin shops on a part-time basis appeared in pre-Revolution times. Tin production reached its apex about 1804, the year before Elias' birth. Tanning surrendered to the more profitable clock making after about 1810.

The City that Could

On January 12, 1772, Elias' great-grandfather, Nathaniel Ingraham, was admitted to the Bristol Congregational Church by letter from Judea. There is apparently no connection between Nathaniel's residence in Bristol in 1772 and that of Elias fifty-five years later.

New Cambridge during the Revolutionary period was the scene of no military battle, though tasting the bitterness of civil conflict. The majority were in favor of the Revolution but the members of the Anglican church led by the Rev. James Nichols were determined Royalists. Chippins Hill was a Tory center where Royalists meetings were clandestinely held.

In 1785 the town was incorporated as Bristol. Nobody knows why the name was changed from New Cambridge. Perhaps it grew from Yankee thriftiness, Bristol being one word instead of two.

Before the War of 1812, Yankees peddled tall clock movements made in Bristol. Junkets were perilous and bizarre. The oncoming demand for clocks was to be felt far and near. Yankee peddlers after 1815 toted shelf clocks, priced within the means of even rural customers.

In 1804, Bristol boasted eleven tin shops, two clock manufacturers, four tanners and shoemakers, two gristmills, three sawmills, two carding mills, four blacksmiths, one silversmith, two merchants, two doctors, one lawyer and several taverns.

By 1815 the village of Bristol ripened for the oncoming clock business which dominated its life for the remainder of the century and beyond. The forest was driven back apace, the community established, mills located. The national life remained settled for the oncoming half century. The thrust began for manufactured products of domestic origin. The great movement of population accelerated westward where manufacturies like clocks were needed.

The old agricultural Bristol changed into its new industrial life, a change following the inertia in the War of 1812 period.

The trickle of tall clocks cascaded into a river of shelf clocks. The surge originating along the banks of the Pequabuck was heard, felt, and seen around the world. The sands of agrarian time ran out as the hourglass of time turned the wheels of industry. "Bristol . . . Bristol . . . Bristol . . . ." Water wheels and clock trains sang a duet of foaming water and striking movements. It's time for time. Note well, dear Bristol, the transition from agriculture to industry . . . . Elias, do you hear this song of time?

Taste now, Bristol, glue instead of syrup. Smell now fir not fur, wood shavings over loam, a factory not a farm, the clock peal above a milk pail, roses as escutcheons rather than flowers. Smell of pine boards not pine needles, patents before potatoes, wood rather than ham curing, cherry in both plank and pie, and factory afire, not the forest.

Hear now, O Bristol, the chatter of bandsaw above bluejay, the whirr of wheels louder than wings, the lyre as wallclock not a harp, harness on both stream and horse; tall clocks over tall tales; warnings from alarm clocks, not just guinea hens; pinion both gear and feather; ticking wood clocks instead of wood ticks; the manager more often than manger.

Feel now, O changing Bristol, precision replacing puttering; dear denoting both cost and affection; verge, an axis and an edge; train, trailing gears, not flowing skirts; mainspring, power supply not a water fount; hands on face as well as wrists; bearings and broaches, both jeweled; leaves as gear teeth not tree fronds; plates, once crockery, now metal; falling weights and fallen trees;

The City that Could

wooden floors once wooded acres; the zest to achieve overriding the struggle to emerge.

See, now, O fair Bristol, joinery displacing husbandry; frieze topping freeze; hammers eclipsing harrows; saws, sod, squares, sickles; pendulums, plows; labels engraved not penciled; arbors, once grape now brass; a second hand instead of secondhand; behold a jig, before a dance now a frame; a scarf, once a woven neck piece now a wood joint; scribe now a scribble, before an historian; a scroll once a parchment, now an ornament; and dovetail more a flaring than plummage; saw horses overriding plow horses; feathering now both in wood and wing; mould, before fungus, now profile; driveway to both dock and stable; and spindles in clocks as well as drays; drums that wind as well as beat; fly, both regulator and insect; cases of clocks as well as for lawyers.

You there, red-headed Elias Ingraham, gifted with mental fiber and moral sinew, you with talent wedded to opportunity, harken to the call to build sawmills not windmills, forges not farms, clocks not barns. Your biography is Bristol's. Your flowering is to be seen the world around in clock and case, and heard in chime and bell. Look up there, Elias Engraham. Listen to destiny's call. Make ready. The rehearsal is past. The curtain parts. You are standing in the wings. Generations are a-comin'.

6

Clocks Eclipse the Sun

4000 B.C.–A.D. 1840

*Were I so tall as to reach the moon
Or grasp the ocean in my span
I am measured by my soul
Mind's the measure of a man.*
  —On Amos Tute's gravestone
     in New England

Earliest man measured time by the changing seasons, the moon's cycles and the interval between sunrise and sunset. Division of time into the more sophisticated segments of hours, minutes, and seconds, "measured duration," came with the development of the knowledge of intervals. All are based on the earth's diurnal and orbital motions.

Ancient people gradually discredited the dogma that the devil was the father of all progress until clockmaking became a safe business. By A.D. 500 the danger of being burned at the stake, stoned, drawn and quartered, hanged, or beheaded for making a clock had lessened.

Early mechanical methods of measuring time were the sand glass, the clepsydra or water clock, and candle-burning. The first clocks may have been the marked shadows of trees resulting in the sundial. Later, hour glasses were

Clocks Eclipse the Sun 63

responsible for the expression, "the sands of time." The water clock was developed to measure time on cloudy days or at night. It was known and used in pre-Christian times by the Chinese, Egyptians, Greeks and Romans. Plato is credited with its invention in 400 B.C.

In the fourteenth century a Frenchman, Henry de Vick, invented a clock with many of the important parts of the modern clock, having wheels, dials, and hour hands. Christian Huygens invented the pendulum by 1657. By 1700 minute and second hands were added to the mechanism. By their genius centuries before, De Vick and Huygens contributed to the success of Elias Ingraham.

Eighteenth and nineteenth century clocks were actuated first by falling weights, later by expanding springs. About 1840 springs replaced falling weights as a source of power and Elias' career gained more momentum because of it.

Early Renaissance-period clocks used the striking of a bell or gong to indicate the hour. The word "clock" relates to the German "glocke." and the French "cloche" both meaning bell.

. . . Our modern clocks and watches have been called the greatest single masterpiece of ingenuity and co-ordinated thought in the history of invention.

Indeed, the social and cultural history of the world may be traced in the development of timekeeping methods, beginning with the first known sundial of some six thousand years ago.

(From *The Romance of Time,* by Brooks Palmer)

Almost the whole of mechanical invention is based upon clock principles. The underlying prescript is the transmission of rotary to reciprocating movement. Gears control the speed mechanism of clocks. This system pervades the greater part of modern machinery, from lathe to auto and from locomotive to phonograph and the style is created by the material, the subject, the time and the man. It is little short of miraculous that a provincial like Elias Ingraham could master as he did such mechanical complexities.

Clocks were expensive in early Colonial times, symbols of prestige in homes of affluent citizens. Like others in rural areas, pioneer Ingrahams told time by noon marks, sun dials, sand glasses, or merely by the sun's position in the heavens. Before 1840 shelf clocks were mostly of wood. The tall or grandfather clock was correlative to the Colonial period and up to the early 1800s. Shelf clocks came into common use after 1815. The era of tall clocks passed before Elias reached Bristol.

Noon marks were in general use even by 1825, when Elias was still an apprentice. In 1811 the Yale College Observatory gave a signal by which a cannon was fired exactly at noon in the New Haven public square so that townspeople could get their noon marks right. In Elias' grandfather's day the custom was to announce the hour of Sabbath service by the beating of a drum. Striking clocks replaced this custom gradually as the eighteenth century advanced.

> . . . Portable sundials were a national forerunner of the personal timepiece. George Washington is said to have carried his pocket sundial frequently in preference to any of the watches that he owned.
> (From *The Romance of Time* by Brooks Palmer)

Indefatigable Yankee peddlers carried and sold clocks far and wide. Foundational to the Bristol clock business were these intrepid peddlers who went from house to

Clocks Eclipse the Sun

house peddling wares, carrying messages, and mail. Most were from Connecticut. The shrewd peddlers generally carried the clock movements only and the local joiners made the cases. When the movement was used alone without any case it was called a "wag on the wall." The clock case and its movement were of equal value in the old, tall clocks. They were usually made during the winter when outside work was impossible. Women earned "pin money" by painting dials, stencilling shelf clock pillars, and decorating the insides of lower clock sashes—pins were dear.

According to a fragmentary 1810 census of manufacturers, clocks made in all of Connecticut numbered 14,569 and were valued at $122,955.

Elias Ingraham heard that the first Connecticut clockmaker was probably Ebenezer Parmele (1690–1777) of Guilford. He made clocks, cabinets and boats. In 1726 Parmele made a tower clock which was installed on the Guilford meeting house steeple. This was the first tower clock in Connecticut, installed in the first steeple of the state. This old clock movement is now displayed in the Guilford Historical Society Museum. In the 1860s Andrew Ingraham lived in Guilford near this old meeting house and saw and heard that old tower clock.

Colonial cabinetmakers made their own tools and worked in poorly heated rooms. Their lumber was first air dried then shed dried, and seasoned in the open beams above the shop. Lumber took a year to dry. Elias didn't make his own tools but even he had to let nature take its course in drying wood.

In the mid-eighteenth century there were at least two American Negro clockmakers, Benjamin Banneker of Baltimore and Peter Hill of Mount Holly and Burlington, New Jersey. There were even women clockmakers: Anna Marie Leroy at work in 1750, Hannah Montenden in 1805, both in Lancaster, Pennsylvania, and Maria Nicollet at work in the 1790s in Philadelphia.

Benjamin Cheney, (1725-1815) of East Hartford near Glastonbury, made brass and wooden movements for tall clocks. John Fitch, inventor of the steamboat, served in his shop as apprentice. Elias' apprenticeship was served a few years after Cheney's death and but a few miles away from his shop.

Enterprising Gideon Roberts (1749-1813) was a Bristol Quaker, choir master, a Revolutionary soldier and once a prisoner on a British prison ship. He made tall clocks with wooden movements, peddling them as far away as Pennsylvania and into the south. He and Eli Terry of nearby Plymouth were the pioneers of mass production of clocks. When Gideon Roberts died of typhus in 1813 he left four hundred movements in process, valued at twenty-five dollars apiece.

Between 1807 and 1810, Eli Terry and Gideon Roberts were the first Americans actually to produce clocks in significant volume. An expert in horological principles, Terry was a master mechanic, a perfectionist and a mechanical genius.

Terry's shelf clock superseded tall clocks. A renaissance in clocks began. Small factories appeared in Bristol. Terry's work and genius, like Elias', were beneficial for generations yet ahead.

The idea of interchangeable clock parts for mass production originated about 1810 either with Gideon Roberts in Bristol or with Eli Terry in nearby Plymouth or with both. This idea whetted consumer appetites for mass produced manufactures and paved the way for a forthcoming prosperous industrial society.

Terry's innovation, the "pillar and scroll" shelf clock, was first sold in 1815. It was fourteen inches wide and four inches deep, had twenty-one inch tapered pillars and

Clocks Eclipse the Sun

square base, a handsome cap, an eleven-inch square dial with a seven-inch tablet of painted glass below. Terry patented this clock case. For a thousand dollars he sold the manufacturing rights to Seth Thomas (1785–1859). This clock, with a one-day wooden movement, sold for fifteen dollars, bringing shelf clocks into thousands of homes previously clockless. Eli Terry and Seth Thomas made fortunes from this clock.

Unschooled Seth Thomas worked for Eli Terry as early as 1808. Thomas, along with Terry and Roberts, became a pioneer in clock mass production.

The only two clock companies founded in the early Bristol clock period that have survived to mid-twentieth century are those of Seth Thomas and Elias Ingraham. Between 1800 and 1820 the transition from the craftsman period to the factory age took place in Bristol as well as in the rest of America.

In 1825 Chauncey Jerome's new case called the "bronze looking glass" provided new impetus to clockmaking in Bristol. Made for a dollar less, it sold for two dollars more than the Terry "pillar and scroll" case. Chauncey had worked for Eli Terry at nearby Plymouth, accounting for similarity in their manufacturing methods. Jerome, like Elias Ingraham, had his eye fixed as much on clock cases as on movements.

In 1824 Noble and Chauncey Jerome formed a clock company with Elijah Darrow, called Jeromes and Darrow. Beginning in 1827 they were the largest manufacturers of clocks in Bristol for the next decade. Their factory stood on the west side of Main Street, north of the bridge.

Fire was the bane of clock factories. It destroyed not only the building and machinery but records as well. Factory fires brought disaster to many a clockmaker, including both Chauncey Jerome and Elias Ingraham.

J. C. Brown (1807-1872), one of Elias Ingraham's early Bristol contemporaries, originated several novel designs—some used by Elias and others for half a century. Brown had a bad fire that virtually ruined him about the time of an Ingraham factory fire in the mid-1850s.

By 1800 wooden movements for tall clocks were made more cheaply than metal ones. The clock market quadrupled. Friction in wooden mechanism was so great that by far the majority of these clocks had only thirty-hour movements. Only a few ran eight days with one winding. In 1837, Chauncey Jerome would hit upon the idea of a one-day clock movement made of brass instead of wood.

> Thare wuz a man in ower toun,
> Hiz naim wuz Mathyu Mears,
> He wound his klok up evry nite
> for twenty-seven yeers.
> Wun da this famus timepiece proved,
> An ait day klok to be,
> An' a mader man than mister Mears
> Yu wood not kair tu see.
>
> Josh Billings

As early as 1811, talented Joseph Ives (1782-1862) made tall clock movements in Bristol. The name Ives became well known among Bristol clockmakers. There were many brothers. In 1831-33 and probably later, Elias made fine clock cases for the Ives, notably for Chauncey and Lawson. J. Shaylor Ives, while working for Elisha Brewster in 1836, patented a brass clock spring. Brooks Palmer says, "Ives was possibly one of the first to devise successful American clock springs." The spring power mechanism rapidly replaced falling weights as power to run clocks.

In 1827, the year of Elias Ingraham's arrival, Bristol

had a population of 1,500 souls. Its manufacturers were already turning out fifty to one hundred thousand clocks annually.

Elias' benefactor, George Mitchell, had a store, ran the post office, and catered to Yankee peddlers. Mitchell itched to introduce a clock superior to the Jerome "bronze looking glass" case. Through his uncle and partner, Alonzo Hinman, he sought Elias Ingraham to design such a case. He found Elias working for Daniel Dewey in Hartford.

The clock case which Elias developed achieved prompt success and gave Chauncey Jerome a run for his money.

7

Forever, My Love

1827–1829

*There is a tide in the affairs of men,
which, taken at the flood, leads on to fortune.*
—Shakespeare

In 1827 spring burst upon New England as in ages past. The upreaching stem, the unfurling leaflet, and the downward groping of root recurred as they had for eons.

Something new that May occurred in Elias Ingraham. Like the green leaflet Elias reached upward, laboring to unfold and, like the rootlet, extending downward, groping to root.

Without a peer in Bristol, George Mitchell was an experienced and energetic businessman. Ever on the lookout to induce craftsmen to settle in Bristol, he brought many a skilled artisan there. He had coaxed the ambitious Chauncey Jerome to town. Mitchell started new businesses and found new markets for Bristol products.

This item was carried in the Bristol *Press* of July 3, 1884:

Mr. Elias Ingraham, who in 1883 wore a sort of beard, a fringe type running below his chin and cheeks, now almost eighty years of age, has prepared a paper for our columns giving the recollections of the business of the town when he came here fifty-seven years ago. It will appear next week.

On July 10, the *Press* carried the following article:

When Mr. Ingraham came to Bristol, Chauncey Jerome and Elijah Darrow were in company, making wooden clocks. Their factory stood on the west side of Main Street, north of the bridge. It has been burned since. They were at that time getting up the bronze looking glass clock, which proved to be a great success, as it was very popular.

Chauncey Ives was making wooden clock movements . . . Mr. Loomis made Mr. Ive's cases by horse power, in a shop near the house of Hon. Tracy Peck, on West street . . . . Mr. Loomis afterward moved to the west.

Chauncey Boardman was making wooden clock movements in Stafford district, East Bristol, for Jonathan Frost, of Reading Mass., who made the cases, and finished and sold the clocks.

Ephraim Downs was making wooden clock movements near where now is Frank Down's grist mill.

Dana Beckwith had a turning shop on the stream back of his house, near what is now called Doolittle's corner, where he made awl handles which he sold to the hardware merchants of Hartford.

George Welch had an iron foundry, where he cast clock bells and weights, as well as other articles. It stood in his meadow on the side of the present National Water Wheel shop . . . .

Elisha C. Brewster was making clock dials of whitewood instead of zinc, the material used now-a-days. He put on a very heavy body of paint, and then rubbed it down to a fine surface. The dials were then lettered and gilded by girls, and when finished were splendid pieces of work. Everything was done by hand. Mr. Brewster lived in the house that Dr. Camp now occupies. His shop stood right west of his house, on the same side of the street . . . . Mr. Brewster was a deacon in the Congregational church, and was the father of N. L. Brewster and the wives of Dr. Camp, Capt. Briggs of New York, and S. P. Newell, Esq., one of our best lawyers.

Ira Ives was running a wood turning shop, since burnt, which stood on the site of E. Ingraham & Co.'s present movement shop. He worked for George Mitchell, who at that time owned the store now occupied by B. A. Hart, where he kept the post office and a dry goods, grocery and drug store. Over this he had a variety store, from which to fit out peddlers. He employed a number of persons to make various articles for this branch of his business. Mr. Ives made a very neat and handsome sandbox of wood, sand being formerly used by writers instead of the blotting paper now common. He also made wooden faucets and dressing combs.

Alanson Richards made brass wire tuck combs. Other parties made mouse traps, tinder boxes, buttons, &c. . . .

Thomas Barnes owned a dry goods and grocery store at the south side . . . .

Barnes' and Mitchell's stores, and the manufactures above mentioned, are the summing up of the old time business of the town when E. Ingraham came here, as he recollects it. Since that time business, and the facilities for doing business, have wonderfully improved in Bristol.

Elias' boss, George Mitchell, had served or would serve as selectman, assessor, school visitor, state assemblyman. A leading spirit in the village, a Baptist, Mitchell was a shrewd trader, a private banker, large land owner. He bought and sold clocks, even made some. As Mitchell's protégé, Elias was in remarkably astute hands, "to work on clockcases one year for one dollar twenty-five cents per day and twelve hours for a day's work," Elias later wrote. About 1825 George Mitchell sold a gristmill and shop

Forever, My Love   73

to Ephriam Downs, 1787–1860, for half cash and half clocks. Writing of Downs, Wallace Nutting in *Furniture Treasury* says, ". . . he made at least two horseback trips to Cincinnati, O., making clocks there for Luman Watson, 1816–21." The forty-year-old Ephraim Downs made clock movements for Mitchell. Elias designed and made clock cases for the Downs wooden movements.

The American Clock Museum of Bristol has a clock with an Ephraim Downs label, handed down in the Ingraham family from among Elias' effects. It answers the description of Elias' first design of a clock case.

This mahogany clock sports hand-carved lion's paw columned feet, ornate carved column caps, a carved front, fretwork at the top, with a carved basket of fruit. It took the public's eye, immediately becoming an excellent seller, jostled Jerome and gave him a run for his money.

Elias first worked by the day for ten and a half cents an hour during his one-year contract with Mitchell. This was a skilled mechanic's wage. In 1829 he made and sold to Mitchell 412 clockcases at $1.25 apiece, 321 in 1830. By hand he made six to eight clockcases a week. Thus his clock case receipts from Mitchell for 1829 were $515, for 1830, $401. He also made and sold furniture and coffins to others.

Elias arrived at a propitious time, finding himself closely associated with founders and promoters of the Bristol clock business.

Bristol's Yankee Peddlers established the outlet for clocks. They went about the nation selling tinware, clocks, leather and woolen goods, furniture and tools among other items. They trekked to the west and the south, to Canada as well. They built up a lucrative business with wealthy southern planters. Until handicapped by expensive peddlers' licenses and later ruined by the Civil War, the best domestic market for clocks was among these planters in the South.

Edward Ingraham II, Elias' great-grandson, once made a study of Elias' first account book. This study sheds light on the business customs of the early 1830s as well as on Elias himself, confirming much of what has been accepted about him.

Elias started the account book after completing his one-year Mitchell contract. The first entry is dated June 28, 1828: "George H. Mitchell to Ingraham and Warren dr. (debtor)." After the caption there are no entries. This suggests that George Warren personally or business-wise was not only associated with Elias but was also indebted to Mitchell. George Warren was an apprentice with Elias, though George was five years older. He may have been married in Farmington about 1830. His son may have been baptized in the Bristol Congregational Church about 1831. After the early 1830s the name "George Warren" flickers then fades into obscurity, while that of Elias Ingraham kindles and flares into eminence for generations to come.

When Elias moved to Bristol many men and women lived a debauched life. Many drank, smoked, chewed and swore. It was common for the abstemious citizens to sign a pledge in which they agreed to abstain from spirituous liquors. A reaction by the pious to the tough times was thus indicated. The temperance movement was launched but the Ingrahams of that period were straight-laced teetotalers already.

With his work day from six in the morning until six at night, Elias had little time for frivolity or carousing, even if he were so inclined. Sundays were days of church-going, discipline, reverence and solemnity.

Like other pious and temperate young men, Elias regularly sabbathed in this stern regimen. And to relieve

Forever, My Love

the severe atmosphere, his thoughts fondly turned towards Glastonbury and his betrothed, Julia Sparks.

See him now that December of 1827 respectfully asking George Mitchell for leave in order to marry Julia. Can't we imagine Mitchell, generous, patronizing, sympathetic, offering Elias whatever time he needed? Would you not expect the fatherly Mitchell to insist that Elias borrow a Mitchell horse and sleigh for his nuptial trip to and from Glastonbury?

Witness Elias Ingraham sleighing the eighteen miles to Hartford, and the nine more to Glastonbury for his tryst. See him drive the borrowed horse and sleigh back towards Hartford from whence but six months earlier he had walked to Bristol.

Hear the crunch of sleigh runners on the rutted road, the squeak of leather traces and the rubbing of the wooden whiffletree against its frigid iron clevis, the labored breathing from red, flaring nostrils of the willing beast. Listen to the murmuring, whispering, sighing of emerald green conifers. Hear the jeering jay, the cawing crow, the ring of an axe in the cold air, the echo of shod hooves and sleigh runners rubbing on the covered wooden bridge over the Connecticut River.

See the shimmering cloud of breath from gelding nostril, the snow-covered rail fences zig-zagging alongside, "horse high, bull proof, and pig tight," the naked grey skeletons of unleafed forest and orchard. Observe the acrobatic nuthatch toe-tipping headfirst down the tree trunk, light snow blowing in fragile flake. Look at swirling wind-blown patches of bronzed leaves, hills with shoulders hunched against winter's onslaught, frozen pond and frigid stream, countryside gripped with icy fingers, barn of chestnut boards painted red, white clapboard farm houses stiff against the cold backdrop of frozen meadow, the heavily-clothed farmer in homespun linsey woolsey at his chores.

Smell the warm, sweaty hair from the flank of the steady trotter, the oily leather of harness and horse collar, fragrant hickory smoke rising from chimney flue.

Sense the glow in Elias' heart, the pang of joy brimming there, the warmth from ear muffs, buffalo robe covering long strong legs. Feel the sway, lurch, and rock of sleigh, the steady pull of black leather reins from bridle bit to mittened sensitive hand, the bite of "flawy" December wind on ruddy cheek and brow.

It is dusk a day or two before Christmas. Mind Julia, near twenty-two, maudlin within her father's Glastonbury farm house, willing, waiting, watching. See her run to meet Elias as he reins in his horse. See him alight from the sleigh. Note how gently he takes her with eager arms. We are certain now that his bachelorhood and her maidenhood are drawing to a close. The wedding is at hand.

Julia's father, Nathan Sparks, was born on October 17, 1774, her mother, Lucinda Hale Sparks, on September 6, 1778. He died young—at 58; she lived to the age of 89.

Nathan's father was Reuben Sparks, a Revolutionary War soldier. Reuben's name appears in a military payroll period covering August 11 to September 30, 1776. He served in Sixth Company under Lt. Stephen Andrus, Sixth Regiment, Col. Chester.

There was a tradition in the Sparks family that they should not inquire too closely into their maternal family ancestry as someone had been hanged. The reference was to Nathan Hale, a collateral relative of Julia's mother. He was hanged by the British as a spy when but twenty-one. Among our country's noblest heroes, Yale educated Nathan Hale was a school teacher when the Revolution

Forever, My Love 77

began. He volunteered as a soldier and was made a first lieutenant. Disguised as a Dutch school master, he entered the British lines to obtain military information. Visiting enemy camps on Long Island and New York, he secured information as to fortifications and other military data. Nathan Hale was captured just as he was planning to return to the American lines. The next morning, September 22, 1776, in New York, Nathan Hale was hanged as a spy in ignominy.

British Major Cunningham denied the condemned patriot's last request for a Bible and destroyed Hale's letters to his friends. Cunningham asked Captain Hale for his last words. His immortal answer was, "I only regret that I have but one life to lose for my country." The British officer then angrily shouted, "Swing the rebel up."

Julia's parents, Nathan and Lucinda were married on December 3, 1797. Julia, born March 27, 1806, was the fourth of their eight children.

Julia's maternal grandfather, Jonathan Hale, married in 1777 his second wife, Mary Clark. Their oldest of eight children was Lucinda, Julia's mother.

The wedding of Elias Ingraham and Julia Sparks took place on Christmas Day, Tuesday evening, December 25, 1827, in Glastonbury. A village record shows that the ceremony was performed by Jeremiah Stocking, Justice of the Peace.

Why were the young people married by a justice of the peace instead of the minister of the Glastonbury church? Elias was still a member there and was until 1832. To be married by his minister would seem to be more appropriate. Among the colonists marriage was a civil contract, though records as early as 1694 indicate ceremonies were sometimes performed by ministers.

Were they married by a justice of the peace because it was Christmas Day? Perhaps. Earlier, Colonial liturgical dissenters had frowned upon celebrating Christmas, considering it a pagan or Anglican holiday. Was there yet a vestige of Calvinism disallowing a wedding ceremony performed by a minister on Christmas Day? Perchance even the minister was away or sick abed or perhaps it was a stormy day . . . .

Had Julia been married before? Here and there a rumor has surfaced in the Ingraham story regarding an alleged previous marriage of Julia's. It is an undocumented allegation. Edward Ingraham II declared that the story about a previous marriage of Julia's exists in neither reliable record nor family tradition.

Here is the rumor. A Julia Sparks Norton is supposed to have been at Martha's Vineyard, in the mid-1820s. The Sparks family is said to have settled there and been interested in the early church on the Vineyard. Elias is supposed to have met Julia there while on a business trip by boat between Hartford and Boston. Stopping at the Vineyard, he is said to have there met and married Julia Sparks Norton. The name "Norton" would imply a previous marriage. Was the Glastonbury ceremony shunned by a minister because a divorced woman was the bride of Elias Ingraham? Records and those informed say no. Martha's Vineyard later enters our Elias Ingraham story, but not in this way.

No one knows who attended this nuptial ceremony besides the bride, the groom, and the worthy Justice of the Peace, Jeremiah Stocking. We surmise that the bride's as well as the groom's parents were there. Eunice and Joseph Ingraham Jr. could certainly have driven up from nearby Marlborough. Andrew would have been there also, if he were at home or nearby. Perhaps Honora, Julia's oldest sister, attended. Some forty years later Honora became Andrew Ingraham's third and last wife.

In the sunset of his life on Christmas Day 1884, Elias wrote a grandson of this ceremony:

> It is some fifty-seven years this evening since I united my destiny with Julia H. Sparks, I have had nothing to start out in life on except a trade which I had served five years apprentice Ship for the Cabinet Business. I had made contract with Geo. Mitchell to work on clock cases one year for one dollar and twenty five per day and twelve hours for a days work. Our boys would think such work pretty hard would they not. To support oneself and wife But the God in whom I trust has blest us in our Business and we have lived happily to geether this fifty seven years and have attained to our present security.

In the summer of 1828 the sloping banks of the Pequabuck River above Bristol were covered with undergrowth, hemlock and hardwoods gracefully bending over the river. Water rushed down a dell between hills. It was a pleasant blending of stream and tree, hill and dale, sweet with an atmosphere of pine, birch and honeysuckle. The river swarmed with speckled trout.

That summer a moderately high dam was built near the bridge. There a current of water turned into a raceway and emptied into a factory pond downstream. From the north side of the village a narrow singing brook united with the raceway supply. A flume gate fed the water from the pond into another raceway to power Jerome and Darrow red clockshops north of the bridge on Main Street. The year before, Jerome and Darrow contracted for 12,000 clocks, an unbelievably large quantity then.

Another dam was constructed a year or two later for the new Jerome factories. A wooden flume two-and-a-half feet wide and three or four hundred feet long was built to carry water direct to the Jerome shops, replacing the original raceway. The rushing current turned a water wheel which provided a direct source of power for the shops. Below the bridge another dam crossed the river providing power to the water wheel for a button factory.

Elias Ingraham on that very wooden rampart on a warm summer's evening schemed his own bridges and clock castles in the air. What he did not dream was that some would crash to the ground.

After the turnpike era came the canal era, then the railroads. Turnpikes were the feeders for the canals, later for the railroads.

Out West Abe Lincoln designed and built a raft. In 1828 at nineteen he floated the raft with produce down the Ohio and into the Mississippi thence to New Orleans. Returning safely by steamer, he handed over to his employer the proceeds of the sale of the raft and the produce.

The Erie Canal was completed in 1825, proving that there was a superior form of transportation to anything previously existing.

A canal was coming close to Bristol. The Farmington, also called the Northhampton, Canal was chartered in 1822. A remarkable engineering feat, it cost two million dollars, a prodigious sum in that day. Traces of the canal remain today.

One month after Elias completed his first contract in Bristol—on Friday, June 20, 1828—a delegation including George Mitchell set out for Bristol Basin and the launching of the first tollpaying boat on the new Farmington Canal. The canal had been cut the sixty miles from New Haven in three years. Mitchell more than anyone else was active in promoting this wonderful new means of transportation.

The canal pushed ahead development of Central Connecticut. Local products found wider markets. Outside goods became available at cheaper prices. More than ever Bristol was a part of the nation. In the early 1840s it became a part of the world as Bristol clocks were shipped abroad.

The same day that work started on the Farmington Canal, the Baltimore and Ohio began construction on the first public railroad in the United States. The roaring railroad era had commenced. Elias beheld the birth of the transportation twins of canals and railroads.

At first most folks considered railroads dangerous. Twelve miles an hour was a wild speed. Engines frightened livestock and kept hens from laying. It was said that the excessive speed would make people go mad. For another reason—competition—canal officials opposed the railroads.

In 1829 a surge of national sympathy by Americans for the Greeks and their struggles began. This sympathy caused a revival of Greek architecture in America. The naming of Ulysses S. Grant reflected this sympathy. Queen Victoria of England was ten, this year of 1829, Robert E. Lee fifteen, Abraham Lincoln twenty, Elias Ingraham twenty-four, Isaiah Rogers twenty-nine.

Isaiah Rogers? He is the architect of the renowned Tremont House opening in Boston this year of 1829.

> . . . Here for the first time was a hotel that broke with all of the old traditions of innkeeping, or crowding the guests into trundle beds, or making them sleep on floors, of courtyards filled with chattering peddlers and creaking carriages, of lobbies which were also barrooms, and room clerks who were also bartenders. It was, indeed, a palace for the people, not only in its elegant structure, its mosaic marble floors, and richly carpeted corridors, its drawing rooms, reading rooms, ladies' parlor, and its decorations in the very latest French taste, but in its treatment of guests as well . . . There were singles and

doubles and no need to brush one's teeth at the pump in the courtyard . . . .

The designer of the Tremont House, and the man who showed America that anyone can have access to a palace, was a Yankee from Marshfield, Massachusetts, named Isaiah Rogers. He was the son of a ship builder and, naturally enough, he apprenticed himelf to a carpenter when he was sixteen and of an age to learn a trade . . . . When the money seemed assured, young Rogers was given the commission to design the Tremont House; it was claimed to be the biggest building in America at the time.

. . . The entrance that Rogers designed for the Tremont House, a Doric portal in the Greek Revival manner that was then the undisputed architectural style for all imposing buildings, became a cliché that hotel builders used nearly everywhere until the 1880s . . . .

. . . He was a staunch Greek Revivalist wherever he went and though he was still building in the 1860s, long after the Gothic Revival had gained ascendancy, he persisted in the manner and style that had made him famous in his youth.

(From *The Tastemakers*, by Russell Lynes)

Into the Ingraham record we enter the architect of the Tremont House because of a striking similarity between Elias Ingraham and Isaiah Rogers. Though five years apart they were carpenter apprentices at sixteen, both became imaginative designers, instructed in drawing during their apprenticeships, both achieved original success while yet in their twenties. The Greek Revival influenced them both. Originators, not imitators, they were nevertheless influenced by the classical as well as by contemporary trends.

Ingraham was the designer of clock cases which set the standard for half of the nineteenth century. Rogers, the father of the modern hotel, established the pattern for

Forever, My Love

imposing buildings in the same era. Both were American tastemakers. Opportunity came to both from seasoned patrons—to Elias from George Mitchell, entrepreneur of Bristol, and to Isaiah from Solomon Willard of Boston, master mason, sculptor, supervising architect of the Bunker Hill Monument.

Isaiah's father, Isaac Rogers, was a clockmaker from 1800 to 1828. Isaiah's grandfather was probably Isaac Rogers (1776–1839), a London master clockmaker of renown. But for the caprice of time, place and circumstance, Elias Ingraham might have designed the Tremont Hotel and Isaiah Rogers, clocks!

8

Graceful Years of Aggrandizement

1828-1833

No man's knowledge here can go beyond his experience.

—John Locke

The decade of the 1830s was the springtime of Elias' business life. His development was varied, rapid. His rising was like the first rank spring growth of alfalfa which contains other than leguminous stalk. The harvest he then garnered was like a first cutting of alfalfa, a mixture of less desirable annuals with the coveted perennial. In that decade he mixed clockmaking with the building of furniture, mirrors, coffins. His later experience of the 1840s with Elisha Brewster and Andrew Ingraham was like a second cutting of an uncontaminated perennial. In the decade of the '40s he made clocks and clocks alone. Not until then did his life work—clockmaking—demand his full attention.

Elias and his partners early adopted a principle, an equation, of supply and demand: a reciprocating equality, where the abundance of the one supplied the need of the other.

Graceful Years of Aggrandizement 85

Elias Ingraham had an innate gift. His ability was uncovered and developed in his apprenticeship. Opportunity now flowed into his life through clocks. Another ingredient—experience—was to temper his character. His iron must become steel, the dross removed.

Julia and Elias boarded for the first year or two of their married life. The entry of April 7, 1829, in his account book indicates that he and Julia commenced boarding with a Mrs. Rich. A fortnight later the book shows a payment for the preceding two weeks in the amount of $5.17.

For fifty dollars a year the Ingrahams rented their first home in September, 1829, from clockmakers Root and Ives. On April 30, 1830, their first and only child, Edward, was born. Like his father, little Edward had blue eyes and reddish hair. We shall know this son as Edward I to distinguish him from Edward II who has helped in the compilation of this book.

The 1830 census shows the Elias Ingraham household to include Mr. and Mrs. Ingraham, their baby son Edward, a boy between fifteen and twenty, and a couple between thirty and forty. Elias himself was twenty-five. The method of census-taking in that period failed to record the names of the household members other than the head of the family. No doubt Julia took in boarders to help support the household and thus early contributed to her husband's substance.

The same census shows George Warren, 30 years old, the head of a household of ten.

After moving to Bristol, Elias became a man of property as tax records witness for various of his early years. In 1828 he paid a poll and military tax of $20 each, plus 36¢, which was six percent of a six-dollar clock or watch. The same appeared in 1829 and 1830.

The period in Bristol of the 1830s was one of small clock enterprises, constantly reorganizing, often failing. In this period Elias Ingraham formed several partnerships pursuant to the business of clock and furniture making. None lasted more than a year or so. Through these associations he expanded his art and skill of developing clocks and learned how to manage men.

From the summer of 1829 through the spring of 1830, he made and sold 733 clock cases for $1,886. In March of 1830 for $11 he built a mahogany bureau for George Warren—the fellow apprentice with Elias who came with him to Bristol from Glastonbury. In May of 1831 Elias' account book has this entry: "Settled all book accounts with George Warren."

Was George leaving town? His name no longer appears on Bristol church roles after 1831. Why did he leave? Nobody knows. Some men, like Elias, become masters while others drift along, satisfied with mediocrity.

Elias filled a large order of furniture in 1830 for Theodore Terry. It was to be charged to his father, Samuel, who was brother and partner of the famous clockmaker Eli Terry. Samuel Terry was both clock and saddle maker. He made clocks for George Mitchell. Samuel's fifth son, Theodore, later had a contract to fashion clocks for P. T. Barnum, the circus wizard.

Samuel Terry had difficulty meeting his $227.84 bill, for Elias entered an account for interest in both 1831 and 1832 against Terry.

In 1830 Bristol's population rose to 1,707. Nearby Hartford, Connecticut's capital, had a population of 9,789. New Englanders this year opposed the federal statute requiring all Indians to be moved west of the Mississippi River. The improvidence of the Cherokee's "Trail of Tears" to the West resulted from this cruel decree.

Son Edward Ingraham I was reared in the tradition of clockmaking. He early showed an interest in his father's

Graceful Years of Aggrandizement

work. Elias' associates greatly loved him as a child. He would one day become active and successful in the clock business and be held in the highest regard. Edward attended school in Bristol and was favored with far more formal education than his father. Rustication shortened his college career at Yale, because Edward never returned following the expulsion.

The salutary provincialism of Elias and Andrew yielded in one generation to a villadom triggered by Edward Ingraham I. The nineteenth century was a century of the incipience of family dynasties in finance and industry—dynasties like the Astors, Vanderbilts, Rockefellers, Du Ponts and to a lesser extent the Ingrahams.

Cracks appeared in the shell of New England religious orthodoxy in the early 1830s. The period of transcendentalism began. That philosophy grew in New England, its outstanding spokesman being Ralph Waldo Emerson (1803–1882) and later Henry David Thoreau (1817–1862). Many transcendentalists were Unitarian ministers who thought the spirit had left the church and that religion needed new vision, new inspiration. They defended the right of each person to follow his own conscience in religious matters. Though their experiments in communal living failed, their philosophy left a lasting impression on ecclesiasticism. There is no evidence that transcendentalism had any visible effect on the religious conventionalism of the Ingrahams who remained stout Congregationalists.

In the 1830s the Victorian Age began, lasting until the turn of the century. The daring of the Elizabethan Period was superseded by the conservatism of the Victorian with its scientific and literary flowering. The swing of the pendulum of one extreme was followed by its swing to another. The Ingrahams partook of this popular conservatism.

The humanitarian movement in America also began in the 1830s. Agitation started against imprisonment for debt, cruel treatment of prisoners and the insane, slavery and slave trade. It championed women's rights, education and freedom of labor. Inventions to free humanity from manual drudgery appeared one after another, including matches, cook stoves, sewing machines, gas, rubber and machinery. Corporations like The Ingraham Company rose to nourish these outreaching human needs.

No clocks labeled Elias Ingraham are known to have existed during the decade of the 1830s. The name Ingraham first appeared on clocks bearing the label "Ray and Ingraham" in 1841. However, that Ingraham was Andrew, not Elias.

Tall clocks with the label "Rueben Ingraham" (1745–1811) are extant. One such is now in the American Clock Museum in Bristol. Reuben was not a direct ancestor of Elias, though their lineage may have been linked.

In 1830 the sensationalism of Circus Master P. T. Barnum appeared in Bristol, exhibiting wax figures in a large hall. A year or two later Barnum returned, holding his show in a big tent displaying elephants, monkeys and other animals that looked like fakes. He used dogs for bears and lions. His humbuggery, alias showmanship, was already evident, though Barnum was yet in his early twenties. The colorful Chauncey Jerome had an unsucessful association with Barnum in a New Haven clock venture in 1855, the same year that Elias Ingraham's Bristol clock shops burned to the ground.

After Elias ceased making clock cases for Mitchell, he had substantial transactions with Chauncey Ives (1777–1857) and his nephew Lawson Ives (1805–1867). Late in 1830 Elias made 200 clock cases for them.

Elias and his partners fashioned the astonishing num-

Graceful Years of Aggrandizement

ber of 5,459 clock cases for C. and L. C. Ives during the three years of 1831-1833. This came to about thirty-five a week. Elias' account book shows that portions of the clock work were sublet to others, a common practice among Bristol clockmakers. He also made cases for Davis and Barbour who peddled their wares in the southern states. Elisha C. Brewster made the movements for the latter firm.

S. B. Jerome described Elias' clock case design of this period as having fluted pilasters on the base, two whole columns in the center with half columns on each side of the dial. The columns were plain, highly polished, carved or gilded finishes, selling for eighteen or twenty dollars.

An item in Elias' account book reads, "to error in charging cash which was interest on note 339.29." This sum indicates large loans or credits by Elias to his customers, probably at pretty stiff rates of interest. Reliable paper money was scarce in the 1830s and "hard money" more so. Barter and notes were still the media for doing business. The nearest bank was in Hartford, eighteen miles away. The only transportation was afoot, by horseback or stagecoach and few traveled to Hartford on just a lark.

On April 18, 1831, Elias bought three acres of land on West Street for $300 from Ira Ives (1775-1848). At twenty-six, Elias was now a land owner. The next month he sold the southern part of his property to L. C. Ives for $150.

In 1831 Cyrus McCormick, a Virginian, twenty-two years old, tried out his reaper. It was among the greatest inventions of all time. It replaced the cradle, a hand instrument for cutting grain.

In 1834 a threshing machine was patented by John and Hiram Pitts of Maine. These harvesters allowed grain crops to be mass produced in the western lands as water wheels enabled industrial crops to be mass processed in the East. Machinery-developed western agriculture helped farmers to afford clocks from Ingraham and other factories of New England.

New markets for Elias and his fellow clockmakers were imperative. Trade routes to the Far East and South America were developing, those to Europe enlarging. Ingraham clocks at this early date were selling around the world and would be for generations to come.

In November of 1831 Elias started his own shop with William G. Bartholomew. For $100 they bought from Ira Ives a piece of land having water privileges on North Street, and erected a cabinet shop. In addition to clock cases they made and sold mirrors, chairs, coffins and other furniture. Elias paid Bartholomew a monthly salary of $25. In 1832 Elias sold his half interest in their shop for $875 and the stock to Jonathan C. Brown (1807-1872). Elias then formed a partnership with Chauncey Goodrich, known as Ingraham and Goodrich. The organization lasted about a year.

The scythe of the Grim Reaper cut down two Ingrahams and one Sparks in 1832. Elias' paternal grandparents Joseph I and Betty Taylor Ingraham died in Marlborough a few months apart. Julia's father, Nathan Sparks, died in nearby Glastonbury.

Nathan Sparks bequeathed one third of his estate to his wife, Lucinda only for the time in which she remained his widow but no longer. He consigned all his household furniture to her forever. He bequeathed $50 to daughter Julia Ingraham and $30 to daughter Honora, later Andrew Ingraham's wife.

The ministers of that period were still strict and austere. They disciplined their members for various types of backslidings. Punishment was rendered for such things

Graceful Years of Aggrandizement 91

as failure to take communion, lying, swearing, drunkenness, fornication, seduction, travel on the sabbath. Charges and confessions were read at church meetings if not during the services. There is no record of any such charges against the Ingrahams of that period or even against any of the early well known clockmakers.

When Elias first attended the Bristol Society, the minister was Rev. Jonathan Cone. During Rev. Cone's ministry the first stir of a temperance movement occurred. Cone preached some temperance sermons and a Congregational group resolved that they would "use no spirituous liquors except in extreme warm, wet or cold weather."

In that day "spirituous liquors" excluded ale, beer, wine or cider. Would we dare ask what weather there is in Connecticut besides "extreme warm, wet or cold"? Even so we doubt if Elias imbibed anything much stronger than water in any season.

> We cold water girls and boys
> Freely renounce the treacherous joys
> Of brandy, whiskey, rum, and gin,
> The serpent's lure to death and sin.
> Wine, beer, cider we detest
> And thus will make our parents blest.
> So here we pledge perpetual hate
> To all that can intoxicate.
> (From *The Making of Bristol,*
> Carleton Beals)

Something more should be said for the intrepid Yankee Peddler. These peripatetics claimed to lubricate their clocks with cricket oil or for their best customers with the oil of bumblebees. These rascals, more mischievous than malicious, had this sort of blithe patter: "Madam, are you in need of any pocket sawmills, horn gun flint, bass wood hams, wooden nutmegs, white oak cheeses, tin bung holes, or calico hog troughs?" They would then list their wares in the wagon: tin and glass ware, mats, brooms, washboards, rolling and clothes pins, utensils, drugs, knives and clocks.

Traveling peddlers sold clocks on twelve months credit. A year later they went over the same ground to secure payment. The clocks sold for two or three times their cost. As long as collections were good, business was good.

The yarns of Yankee Peddlers are legion and amused Elias Ingraham, tickling his typically restrained and disciplined dry Yankee sense of humor. The peddlers boasted of having clocks that ticked loud enough to scare away rats, razors so keen that if you but stropped them and put them under your pillow, you'd wake up clean shaven!

One Connecticut shoemaker bought some wooden shoe pegs made of rotten wood. Unable to use them, he took his knife, sharpened the other end of them and sold them for oats.

One story is about a peddler who always sold a clock with the understanding that he would return in a few weeks, and if the clock did not run satisfactorily he would replace it. He sold all his clocks but one, and when reaching the end of his route, turned back with his one remaining clock. Returning to the house where a clock he had sold did not run, he replaced it with the one remaining clock. At the next house he replaced an unsatisfactory clock with the one he had just taken from the first house. And so he went on, selling and replacing clocks, waxing fat on the proceeds all the while!

The Yankee Peddler was brought up in a hard land and climate with a middle class mercantile heritage. Ingrained habits of thrift, diligence and handiness produced an industrious and restless stock of whittling, spin-

Graceful Years of Aggrandizement 93

ning, contriving, swapping Yankees. They spilled over into roads and ocean lanes of commerce while home craftsmen streamed into factories.

Perpetual motion was incarnate in Yankees with their ingenuity in making and placing manufactures. They followed the fringe of settlement pursuing their livelihood, actively extending the frontier. The original Yankee Peddlers lasted until the Civil War. They moved into the South like a pestilence. They were accused of having the grip of a crab and the suction of a mosquito. They could not be denied, insulted or fatigued. They could be dismissed only with a purchase. Like migrating birds, they worked the south in winter, the north in the summer. Often their wagons contained $1,000 to $2,000 worth of merchandise. They stood picturesquely halfway between a merchant and gypsy. Many of Elias' early clocks were sold by such intrepid Yankee Peddlers.

On February 13, 1833, wedding bells rang for farmer Andrew Ingraham and Lucy Finley, two years his senior. Their marriage was childless, ending tragically four and a half years later. Lucy died in Bristol at the age of thirty-two. Andrew and Lucy had apparently been married at Marlborough, for in May 1837, they both had joined the Bristol Congregational Church from the Marlborough parish. In 1836 Elias coaxed his brother to Bristol where there was plenty of work in the blossoming clock industry.

S. B. Jerome says that Elias Ingraham organized a knitting company in Bristol. Elisha Brewster and John Birge companioned Elias in the new enterprise called Bristol Knitting Company. When the firm was formed, John Birge asked his son, N. L. Birge, who was in California, to return and take an interest in the business. N. L. Birge and Chauncey Sparks were then admitted to the company. The business was just started when the heavy rain of November, 1831, broke the reservoir, tore away the west abutment and a portion of the dam. It took three months to repair the damage. The embankment was then swept away a second time. This was in March, 1832, and a gang of men in the charge of Mr. Ingraham were employed until May to make repairs. Even so, the enterprise was a success. This knitting business became known after Elias sold out as N. L. Birge and Son. Knitting was not to be his cup of tea, although Julia may have drunk deeply of it at home.

In 1833 the firm Ingraham, Bailey and Company was formed. Beginning in February of that year, Elias' account book recorded many somewhat insignificant entries regarding this partnership, mostly "horse baiting and travel"—horse baiting meaning the feeding and care of horses. The partnership was one largely of livery work though petty sales are listed of lumber, clock cases and parts.

Elias evidently prospered and became a man of means, judging from the 1833 assessment. He paid $36.96 tax on a fifty dollar clock or watch. He paid poll tax on a $1,100 house. He was also assessed for $100 worth of land, an $80 horse and a $75 carriage. In addition, Elias paid taxes on his business assets equal to or more than his personal taxes.

The next year his horse was assessed at $10 less, his carriage $30 less. *'Pears that the Ingraham horse and carriage were being run around some, Elias. Pretty busy? The horse and carriage disappear from the assessment records of 1834. Were your Julia and little four-year-old Edward then afoot, Elias? Did you wear out that old horse and carriage so soon?*

We conclude this account book survey by listing some, by no means all, of Elias' delightful spelling, indicating his limited formal education:

Graceful Years of Aggrandizement 95

. . . Ballance . . . contarrary . . . Mahoggany . . . barels of sider . . . ceeping hors . . . teem wagon . . . Hous . . . cain seet shairs . . . wood seet chairs . . . peises . . . cubbord . . . common bedsted . . . French bedsted . . . Wrighting desk . . . wate paterns patterns for clock weights . . . Linnen . . . callicow . . . shoos panterloons . . . surkular saw . . . partatoes . . . Brekfirst table . . . dew on the ould account . . . hedbord . . . Brex fist table . . . mahogany front bearu.

The following items he not only made and sold, but spelled correctly:

. . . childs chair 63¢ . . . large rocking chair upholstered 6.00 . . . cherry coffin 4.00 . . . coffin for Mary Norton 5.00 . . . coffin for child 3.00 . . . cherry coffin for child 6.00 [funeral expenses have risen in the last century] . . . Dressing table 1.25 . . . Dining table 9.63 . . . Secretary and book case 35.00 . . . clothes chest 3.00.

Anyone for furniture in the 1830s?

Edward Ingraham II observes:

Curiously the bulk of the entries are for the years 1831–32–33. What happened after that? There are enough blank pages in the book to allow Elias to continue these accounts for several years. Did he start a new book—long lost? Did someone else (a partner, perhaps) keep the books? It is unthinkable that he was inactive and idle. Most of these accounts illustrate the swapping and trading which occurred.

9

Bristol Clocks in Every Quarter

1835-1839

Do not bring me your successes for they weaken me. Bring me your problems for they strengthen me.
—Charles Kettering

In 1835 Bristol, Connecticut, built a little white schoolhouse on South Street. Atop it was a cupola with a high-keyed, clear-toned, swinging bell. Little Edward Ingraham likely attended this one-room school. He must have looked out its north windows at a boggy pasture strewn with boulders as tall as six feet. A well worn path led down to a stream which found its way from Fall Mountain after many windings to the Pequabuck. At recess on warm days boys waded the stream, often crossed it to pick blackberries growing on a flat sandy lot yonder.

School children sometimes flocked across the roadway to listen to fiddler Sherman Treat. Three or four rods south of Sherman's house lived his brother, Barzillai, a musician and skilled mechanic. He built for Chauncey Jerome a large first-class pipe organ for which Elias

The famed mahogany "Sharp Gothic" clock case, fashioned by Elias Ingraham on board a sailing ship returning from South America about 1843, has been called a "Son of Elias" to illustrate the early genius of the Bristol craftsman.

This Pillar and Scroll clock *(left)* was an Eli Terry invention produced in Plymouth, Connecticut about 1818. The clock had an outside escapement. Terry started mass production of shelf clocks soon after the War of 1812. When this Bronze Looking Glass Clock *(right)* was produced by Jeromes & Darrow about 1827, George Mitchell hired Elias Ingraham to design a clock to compete with it. Jerome's clock is on display in the American Clock and Watch Museum at Bristol, Conn.

In 1828, Elias Ingraham had this design ready for George Mitchell's inventory to compete with Jeromes & Darrow's Bronze Looking Glass Clock. This clock, labeled Ephraim Downs, is on display in the American Clock and Watch Museum at Bristol, Conn. The personal clock of Elias Ingraham, it was handed down to a grandson.

(top) On June 19, 1885, approximately two months before he died, Elias Ingraham loaned three of his earliest clocks to the Bristol Centennial Loan Exhibition. This display was a popular one because of the city's extensive contribution to the clockmaking industry. *(bottom)* This copy of a line engraving, etched in steel, is taken from the Connecticut Historical Collections, by John Warner Barber. It was published in 1837, and shows at top right the new Congregational church which Elias Ingraham helped to build.

Elias Ingraham *(right)* in early manhood, painted by an itinerant artist about 1836. *(left)* Julia Sparks Ingraham was painted also by an itinerant artist in 1836, when she was about 30 years old.

Andrew Ingraham, *(left)* as painted by an itinerant artist in 1837. *(right)* Elisha Curtis Brewster (1791-1880) holds a grandchild. Brewster joined the Ingraham brothers as a partner in 1844 to launch a lucrative clockmaking business that lasted until about 1852.

The Hayes' Patent "premium rocking and reclining" chair enterprise diverted Elias Ingraham from clockmaking and led him into bankruptcy. Elias learned his lesson in the late 1830s and never left clockmaking again.

PREMIUM ROCKING & RECLINING CHAIR

HAYES' PATENT—made by E. Ingraham, Bristol, Conn. For sale in this city only by the subscriber, and at the manufacturer's lowest prices.

D. S. DEWEY.

128 Main street, July 7. 5d 1w

NOTICE.

EXCHANGE BANK, Hartford, July 2, 1838.

A Dividend of three and a half per cent. for the last six months, has been declared on the capital stock of this Bank, payable on and after the 10th inst.
3w33 3d   ELISHA COLT, Cashier.

CON. RIVER BANKING CO.
JULY 2, 1838.

A DIVIDEND has this day been declared on the capital stock, payable to stockholders on the 10th instant.   33   H. ALDEN, Cashier.

Joseph Ingraham (1776-1858), father of Elias and Andrew, was photographed with what appears to be a wig in Ohio where he undoubtedly was visiting his brother. Joseph was born four days after the signing of the Declaration of Independence.

(top) Pictured beside this "Doric" clock is the bottom of the drawer from a drop-leaf table on which Elias Ingraham designed the case. The table was owned by Edward II and is now on display in the American Clock And Watch Museum, Bristol, Conn. *(bottom)* The "Venetian" (No. 1) model bears the label of Elias Ingraham & Co. (1859-1861). It was patented with its circular doors and rosettes by Elias in 1857 and provided a basic model for the Ingraham firm until discontinued in 1877. The Venetian is one of about 1,000 clock cases which Elias designed. The author has one in his home.

Employees of the E. Ingraham & Company, about 1878, posed in front of the Movement Shop at North Main Street in Bristol. The Victorian House at the left was originally used as the Brewster and Ingrahams office. It was razed in 1975.

The final home of Elias and Julia Ingraham at North Street and Burlington Ave., Bristol, Conn., was torn down in 1938 to make way for a gasoline station. The author describes the contents of this house in detail as they existed at the death of Elias Ingraham, having obtained the inventory from old city records.

Elias Ingraham in late years, photographed at Martha's Vineyard, Mass., where he regularly retreated to escape Bristol's summer heat and mosquitoes.

Julia Sparks Ingraham outlived Elias by nine years. This photograph was also taken in Martha's Vineyard, near the Gothic cottage which Elias owned as a vacation home.

The lifetime of Edward Ingraham I *(center)*, the only son of Elias and Julia, marked the disappearance of provincialism in this Ingraham line. Educated at Yale, Edward I administered his father's clockmaking enterprise successfully and died in 1892, seven years after the passing of his father. Walter Andrew Ingraham (1855-1938) *(below left)* succeeded his father Edward I as president of the Ingraham firm. Elias and Julia took grandson Walter at the age of three when his father was in Chicago seeking recovery of health and raised him to adulthood. *(below right)* William Shurtleff Ingraham (1857-1930) succeeded his brother Walter as president of the Ingraham Company. He was the father of Faith, Edward II, and Dudley Ingraham, and the grandfather of the author's wife, Jean Treadway Holly.

A page from the account book of Elias Ingraham itemizes work done for C & L C Ives in 1831, and money owed for each of the twenty-one items.

Messrs C & L C Ives   Dr
                                                    $ Cts
1831
Dec 26th   To 64 ft Pine Plank   2   7
            To making 1 Box & Box 1 Clock   000 17
    29th   To Hills labor on half Day   000 62½
    31st   To making wale Paterns   000 50
Jan 3d   To Halls labor making box Paterns varnish 0 94
    5th   To the use of Mr Mitchills veneering   0 34
    11th   To setting window glass   000 17
    26th   To 102 Looking G Cases for wood @ .75   85
Feb 1st   To 52½ ft Pine Plank   1 07
    2nd   To making 104 House hd cases @ .136   141 44
            To turning & mending Sash for R M   2 5
    15th   To 50 Gilt Cases for Brass 6 ft (53)   76 50
            To Wm Hills labor 22 Days @ 1.34   29 48
            To Pine for whors 21½   000 64
            To Cherrey Board for veneering 7 ft   00 42
March 10   To Hills fixing stove   000 97½
    19th   To Pine white oak Plank   000 8
    23d   To 151 New fashion Cases @ 1.10   166 10
            To New modling over a new fashion   000 75
April 18th To Hills labor making frames Saws   5 36
    25th   To 305 Looking Glass Cases 94c   286 70
                                                   $809 26

Edward Ingraham II, *(left)* retired as president of the company after serving in that capacity from 1927 to 1954. He died in 1972 inside the American Clock and Watch Museum of Bristol during a discussion with the curator. Mr. Ingraham served as a valued collaborator in the preparation of the Elias Ingraham story. *(right)* Dudley S. Ingraham of Litchfield, Conn., younger brother of Edward II, served as president of the family company from 1954 until 1956.

Bristol Clocks in Every Quarter

Ingraham made a handsome, solid mahogany case, said to be the largest and finest piece of cabinet work ever built in Bristol to that time. The organ was loaned and placed in the Congregational Meeting House until 1846, when the bumptious Chauncey Jerome removed it.

At about the time little Edward started to school, Elias and fifteen other clock manufacturers in Bristol had made clocks valued at a million dollars. Clock production had increased fifty times in eighteen years.

Clock materials came from some distance, often overland: brass from Waterbury and Wolcottville; nails, screws, wire, glass, and glue from Hartford; mahogany, varnish, oil and turpentine from New York; and pine from Albany, New York, Maine and New Brunswick. Ten to twenty horses were at work for each important factory. When the canal was inoperative a team took an entire day to travel thirty miles to New Haven, often a Herculean task for man and beast through storms and rain and snow over rutted roads. Pig iron, scrap iron, and coal came to Bristol by canal. Coal came in forty or fifty pound lumps, which were hammered and cracked at foundries before being used in furnaces.

The Ingrahams in the 1830s paid prices like these: haircuts, 12½¢; a 2½-lb. sirloin steak, 30¢; a hired girl for a week, $1.50; weekly board for a single man, $2 to $2.25. Craftsmen worked ten to twelve hours a day, six days a week, for an hourly 12½¢. Unskilled workers earned less.

About the year 1835 Southerners began to oppose Yankee peddlers selling Northern wares in the South. Laws were passed requiring peddlers' licenses so expensive as to constitute a near prohibition of the sale of clocks made out of state.

With typical Yankee ingenuity, shrewd New England clockmakers defined the word "made" as meaning "finished." At once they packed up clock movement parts, shipped them to the South, took along workmen who assembled the parts into finished clock movements. They doubtless shipped some clock cases to the south into which movements were introduced but some clock cases were also made in the South.

On September 21, 1835, thirty-year-old Elias purchased from Josiah Davis, Jr., for $2,300 two-thirds of an acre and a turning shop together with water privileges. This property was bounded on the west by a passway, now North Main Street, and on the east by a brook. Elias paid for the property in finished clock case parts ready to ship to Davis and Barbour in Macon, Georgia, where they were assembled, peddled and accepted as a locally manufactured item.

Following his early training, Elias had made not only clock cases but furniture as well, since his new skills exceeded his clock case business needs. Like many another eager young businessman, he was about to overextend himself, ignorant of an oncoming business depression.

The 1835 Elias Ingraham assessment included: one house, $1,100; two acres of land, $200; two timepieces, $14; manufactures, $1,100; poll, military and occupational taxes, all amounting to $152.84 tax. For a young man he was coming up fast in the world.

In 1835 the first railroad was built between New Haven and Hartford via nearby Berlin. Stagecoach service began from Bristol to Berlin nine miles away. For the first time it was now possible for Elias to go to New Haven and back in a single day, a round trip of 60 miles. Imagine such progress!

Due to the ingenuity of Joseph Ives, since 1832 eight-day brass weight-driven clock movements were made proving more dependable than the cheaper wooden ones then on the market. After 1837, Jerome's one-day brass

Bristol Clocks in Every Quarter

weight-driven movement gradually drove out the wooden movement. The change from wood to brass shook up the entire clock industry. Great stocks of wooden clocks were junked. At one factory two thousand were piled up with no takers. Contemplate what a scramble there would have been for those wooden clocks had the date been moved to the antique-hungry mid-twentieth century!

The oncoming five-year depression beginning in May and June of 1837 brought confusion and disenchantment to struggling clockmakers, including Elias Ingraham. Bankruptcy and reorganization were the rule rather than the exception. Elias would find himself among those who failed in business because of inexperience, lack of capital, and a national condition beyond his control. Only two or three well capitalized clock concerns changed over quickly from wooden to brass clocks. They scarcely faltered. Unfortunately, Elias stumbled.

A debtors' prison was not uncommon and at least one Bristol clockmaker did not escape it. Among the cleverest clock geniuses Bristol ever produced, Joseph Ives was nevertheless a rather poor business man. In the early 1830s he landed in a Brooklyn debtors prison, locked up with murderers, thieves and degenerates. John Birge (1785-1862), an important and successful Bristol wagon builder and clockmaker, bailed him out.

Elias' fate in the early 1840s was less doleful than that of Joseph Ives but still cheerless. It would be Elias' brother Andrew who bailed him out of his impoundage, as the story shall relate.

As Bristol clock pendulums swung into multiple rhythm, the pendulum of industrial evolution increased its tempo. The wave of political revolution of the late 1700s was followed by the rise of industrial evolution. Mechanization and capital would merge with science, resulting in better products for less money. Water current, wind, animal and human muscle as sources of power gave way to mechanical engines. Faster transportation shrank the globe through more and better roads, turnpikes, canals, railroads. The oceans narrowed as crossing quickened. As means of communication accelerated, more and better timekeeping was necessary. Elias was about to falter but would soon recover into quickened and more purposeful clockmaking.

The transition was steady following the War of 1812 and hastened after the Civil War. The whole way of living was altered, changes came thick and fast as invention and mechanization gained interest and fruition. Science converging with industry elevated, refined and extended human effort, making it more efficient and productive. Speed on land, water and in men's affairs accelerated human pace. Inventions were so frequent during the 1800s that some deluded men wanted the patent office to close because there was "no more to be invented."

In 1836 Elias' assessments paralleled those of the previous few years. He was assessed $30 as a mechanic, a form of income tax, paying a total tax of $121. The assessment for mechanics was significant. It ran from $10 for small concerns to $300 to $400 for opulent men like Chauncey Jerome.

While Elias was establishing himself as a Bristol clockmaker, his brother Andrew had been a moderately successful farmer. Andrew had married into an old Marlborough family. He and his bride moved from Marlborough to Guilford, Connecticut, where they resided for a time.

Accepting Elias' invitation to come to Bristol, Andrew purchased on February 27, 1837, a house and land on West Street for $1,600. Paying $200 down, he gave his note for $1,400. Elias as co-signer for Andrew indemnified the mortgage. Little did either know of the oncoming national depression. Three years hence Andrew more than reciprocated this fraternal support when Elias was in a financial crisis.

For the next three years Andrew worked for his older brother in one way and another. A farmer, he was not a trained mechanic or craftsman.

By letter from the Marlborough Society, Andrew and his wife, Lucy, on May 7, 1837, joined the Bristol Church Society. On September 30 that year, tragedy struck the Andrew Ingraham household. Lucy Finley Ingraham, his wife of only four years, lay dead at thirty-two years of age. Nothing more is known of her or of the circumstance which caused her death. That Andrew grieved we are certain. That Elias consoled him we are sure.

Andrew was indeed a brother to Elias both in the family and from the heart. For twenty years Andrew faithfully worked with Elias in the clock business. They understood, helped, encouraged and supported one another.

Andrew came when called. Elias finally reached a point when it was time to carry on with his son, Edward. Andrew then gradually faded from the clockmaking scene. He reentered the business later, albeit without significance. It is ironic though entirely fitting that in 1841 the first known Ingraham clock label bore Andrew's, not Elias' name. However, there would be plenty of exposure for the elder brother as well on notable clocks in the generations still ahead.

Andrew possessed many appealing qualities. With little formal schooling, he evidenced attributes of indefatigability, gentleness, courage, sincerity, piety. Thrice a widower, sadly he would remain childless. He had less of earthly joys and success than Elias. Like his brother, Andrew had a quiet religious zeal. Both had more backbone than jawbone.

After nine months' bereavement, on June 6, 1838, with typical Ingraham resilience, the taciturn Andrew married Rhoda Barber, daughter of Gideon Barber, Jr., of Barkhamstead, Connecticut. A spinster until thirty-two, one year his senior, she remained his beloved wife for the next thirty-six years. Gideon Barber, Jr., Ingraham's father and grandfather, had been Revolutionary War patriots.

A wave of speculation and reckless expansion was sweeping the nation in 1833. The situation was complicated by the failure of certain great financial houses in England which had invested heavily in American securities, by crop failures in the West, and by President Jackson's 1836 circular requiring public lands to be paid for in "hard money."

Wild land speculation based on easy bank credit swept the west until halted by the panic. Hundreds of banks failed, unemployment was serious in towns and cities, including Bristol, speculators lost their lands, railroad and canal construction virtually ceased. Financial stringency prevailed everywhere in this national industrial depression.

Southern states sold their products to Europe and were paid in "hard money." Clocks had moved well to the planters until this depression. Then the southern business fell flat on its clockfaces.

By 1837, economic panic had hit Bristol clockmakers hard. About two-thirds of them went bankrupt. Even the veteran George Mitchell found himself insolvent.

The depression, coupled with the innovation of one day weight-driven brass clock movements, dealt a severe blow to the traditional wooden clock movements. Everything that had been wrong with wooden clocks was exaggerated. They were no better, it was said, than wooden nutmegs

Bristol Clocks in Every Quarter   103

and wooden cucumber seeds. They couldn't be successfully shipped by water. The works swelled in damp weather. They were said to be a delusion and a snare in a beautiful case.

The darkest hour preceded the dawn. This axiom was now demonstrated in the resourceful, torrential nature of Chauncey Jerome. A new idea popped into his head.

> The hard times came down on us and we really thought that clocks would no longer be made. Our firm thought we could make them if any body could, but like the others felt discouraged and disgusted with the whole business as it was then. I am sure that I had lost, from 1821 to this time, more than one hundred thousand dollars, and felt very much discouraged in consequence. Our company had a good deal of unsettled business in Virginia and South Carolina, and I started in the fall of 1837 for those places. At Richmond I was looking after our old accounts, settling up, collecting notes and picking up some scattered clocks.
>
> One night I took one of these clocks into my room and placing it on the table, left a light burning near it and went to bed. While thinking over my business troubles and disappointments, I could not help feeling very much depressed. I said to myself I will not give up yet, I know more about the clock business than anything else. That minute I was looking at the wood clock on the table and it came into my mind instantly that there could be a cheap one-day brass clock that would take the place of the wood clock. I at once began to figure on it the case would cost no more, the dials, glass and weights and other fixtures would be the same, and the size could be reduced.
>
> . . . I called on the Connecticut men who were finishing wood clocks for that market and told Mr. Dyer, the head man, that I had got up, or could get up something when I got home that would run out all the wood clocks in the country, (Seth) Thomas's and all; he laughed at

me quite heartily. I told him that was all right, and asked him to come to Bristol when he went home and I would show him something that would astonish him. He promised that he would, and during the next summer when he called at my place, I showed him a shelf full of them running, which he acknowledged to be the best he had ever seen.

(From *American Clock Making,* Chauncey Jerome)

Jerome's idea to build a brass one-day clock, if indeed it was his idea, was at least the falling apple that wakened him and other clockmakers to a new and prosperous era. He had spawned an idea, the issue of which finally circled the globe and accrued even to the benefit of Elias Ingraham.

The Jerome talisman in 1837 revolutionized the clock industry, just when needed to stimulate the falling markets. This thirty-hour brass clock superseded the one-day wooden movement and because of low cost competed with the eight-day brass conceived by Joseph Ives. Jerome's new brass style sold for a lower price than any ever produced in Europe or America. This style really brought clocks to the average man's price range. Clocks with brass movements soon sold by the hundreds of thousands.

The making of brass movements took considerably more capital than wooden movements. Increased output and wider markets were now necessary. This transition occurred at the first low point of Elias' career.

Within twenty years substantially all the common clocks made in the United States were of rolled brass. By 1855 four clock manufacturers alone would have a combined production of four hundred thousand a year. Clocks with wooden movements gradually became collectors' items.

After the War of 1812 the domestic brass industry progressively gained supremacy over foreign brass. New brass clock movements stimulated the brass industry in Bristol. These new metal clock movements at first must have seemed alien to Elias who so loved working with wood. A succession of inventions in the clock industry in the late 1830's and in the 1840's brought a transition not only from wood to metal for movements but also from falling weights to springs for power. Clocks thus were reduced in size and price and could be placed on a shelf instead of the floor or the wall. Accompanying this change in the mechanism came the change of design to attractive small cases for shelf clocks. Elias Ingraham contributed much to this change in clock case design.

The light of the industrial revolution flickered, burst into flame. The backbone of the American Industrial economy was forged. Terrys, Ives, Jeromes, and Ingrahams now played a significant part in a clock renaissance.

During this tumult Elias saw the logic that one company should make both cases and movements, thus producing a complete clock under one roof. Himself a seasoned case designer and maker, he would associate himself with another man, Elisha C. Brewster (1791–1880), experienced in brass clock movements and springs.

The period between 1837 and 1843 was for Elias one of unrequited toil, financial reversal, bankruptcy, a year's absence, inspiration, transition and finally reinstatement. His promising career was immersed but not drowned. His character and manhood were tested, quickened, molded. His native Yankee mental sinew and moral fibre were stretched and strengthened. The years of torpor broadened his outlook, matured his judgment, and desire quickened his talent.

Craftsmen, trained in the old school as cabinet makers, could plane a rough sawn board to uniform thickness, make a paneled door, lay out and make stair treads of any pitch, or build a spiral staircase. Men of their training designed and built a house to the last detail, put in a paneled room with carving, made a highboy, a bureau or chair. They could join edges of two boards as neatly as a modern planing machine or make moldings for picture frames. All these and more were the skills of old time craftsmen like Elias Ingraham who now wandered off the beaten clock path into one of a patented chair.

Edward Ingraham II writes, "Yesterday I ran across a silver medal (long in my possession) awarded by the Mechanics Institute of New York with the following inscription, 'Awarded to E. Ingraham for a patent easy chair September, 1839.'" The "E" had to be Elias and the chair the Hayes patent—Patent Invalids or Easy Chair.

That Elias was afield from clock case making is seen from three old letters. The first, dated March 14, 1837, was written by eighteen-year-old Hiram Roberts to his brother, George H. Roberts:

> Father says he intends moving back to Bristol again this spring, in the course of a month or two. Mr. Jerome wants to have him come, to make wagons, but he has not decided what he shall do. Mr. Ingraham is making an easy chair, which can be turned into a bed, chair or sofa, as quick as a ventriloquist can make a lady appear in a piece of pie. It beats everything else all hollow, and I expect by the noise it makes . . . . Mr. Ingraham wants to have Father take the agency of it, and offered him fifty dollars a month; but he does not think he shall.

That Titus Roberts changed his mind is witnessed by this second letter dated September 4, 1837, from Lucia P. Roberts to George H. Roberts:

> Your Father is in Mr. Ingraham's employ at fifty dollars a month for the present, and gone for most of the time.

He expects to go to New York in about two weeks, unless they are successful in raising money, and will probably be there a while with you.

That Elias was right serious about this patented chair is demonstrated in this third letter dated also September 4, 1837, from Titus Roberts to his son George in New York:

Mr. Ingraham seems anxious I should continue in his employ, & make a trial in New York, and he is making 2 or 3 splendid chairs, to exhibit at the meeting of the Mechanics Institute on the 25th, and the American Institute a few days after, and it is possible I may continue in N.Y. through the winter.

The silver medal awarded to Elias Ingraham occurred just two years after Titus Roberts showed Elias' patented chair at a meeting of the Mechanics Institute. A few months later the silver lining had a cloud.

Ingraham, Elias: Fancy chair, mirror, and clockcase maker, Bristol, Conn., 1830's. Made Haye's patented easy chair, a combination rocker and bed chair.
(From *Antique Chairs,* by Carl Dreppard)

In 1836 Josiah Peck was the Bristol agent for the Benjamin F. Hayes patented easy chair which could be variously positioned for sitting, reclining or rocking. Two sets of rockers enabled the chair to be a rocker or a cradle. It was thought salutary in the case of sickness.

Encouraged by physicians and townspeople, Elias was convinced it was a good thing and naïvely took hold of the manufacturing of the chairs, some of which were marketed by Daniel Dewey of Hartford, in the same shop where Elias spent the last year of his apprenticeship.

The wave of speculation that rolled across the nation in the thirties soon washed over Elias. He found that some of his optimistic thoughts were not his own but rather the backwash from the tide of speculative human affairs.

Finishing a clock case contract with a Mr. Davis, Elias dropped clock case making and concentrated on the patented Hayes chair with Yankee determination and Ingraham energy. He expected chair-making to be more lucrative than clockmaking.

As in many another new enterprise, he encountered unlooked for obstacles and expenses. The chair undertaking was unsuccessful, even catastrophic for Elias.

He sank into the quicksands of want. He was finding that salt, not sugar, toughens the hide.

Early in 1840 Elias reached the end of his rope, irretrievably extended to bankruptcy. Would he bend willow-like under the storm of adversity or like the rigid oak, break? Were his desire, his drive, his courage gone, his nerve frayed, his faith shaken? Would faltering be prolonged, momentary, or not at all? Why did he sail away to Caracas during this tempestuous period of reversal?

Elias, like an unwound clock, had run down for a spell. Like a clock rewound he would with his brother Andrew and Elisha Brewster in 1843 restart the Ingraham pendulum oscillating. Like his beloved Pequabuck he coursed along, seeking his own level, his own route, his own outcome, awaiting the clearing of the stream, knowing he would not lose the way for the winding. Soon adversity opened his inner eye and unstopped his inner ear. From intuitional depths he was soon to raise to reality a clock design hitherto unequalled in beauty and character.

10

Bankruptcy!

1840-1844

If a man does not keep pace with his companions, perhaps it is because he hears a different drummer. Let him step to the music which he hears, however measured or far away.

—Thoreau

The die was cast. On January 10, 1840, Elias gave an $8,000 mortgage deed to the benevolent Chauncey Ives to all his property on West Street and on both sides of North Main Street!

> . . . together with my dwelling house and all out buildings all factory buildings and machinery among which is engine lathe, veneering saw and frame, three saw frames with the saws and frames, four stoves and all the pipes in the factory, two drill lathes, also the following articles of household goods, one mahogany bookcase and bureau, twelve cane seat chairs, one set of wood chairs, mahogany rocking chair, one carpet, one clock and case two bedsteads French two beds and all bedding belonging thereto, one gilt looking glass.

Now bankrupt, the next day Elias assigned to Chauncey Ives all of his property "upon trust and confidence that he will sell and dispose of the same under the direction of the Court of Probate according to law and said Ives to apply the avails of said premises when sold to and among all my creditors in proportion to their several claims against me."

The Probate Court appointed fellow clockmakers Chauncey Jerome, Ransom Mallory and William Darrow commissioners to list all assets of and claims against Elias. The list in the commissioners' report partially discloses the extent and nature of Ingraham's business. Elias' patented chairs, the Hayes "marvel" to be sold by Titus M. Roberts, numbered 129 in various stages of completion. That he worked with varied components was clear from the references to 128 levers, 137 arbors, ketches, bushings, bearings, 96 pitman connection rods, polished trimmings and brass knobs. That Elias also did upholstery is indicated by the inventory of hair cloth, curled hair, and 85,000 tacks. Additionally were such miscellaneous items as turpentine, glass, varnish, turkey boxwood, picture and mirror frames, iron and brass wire and tubing, lumber including mahogany, hickory, white wood, black walnut, cherry, chestnut, hemlock; wirecutting shears, three work benches, machine for putting chairs together, writing desk, one horse and wagon, buffalo (doubtless robe rather than beast), an easy chair supposed to be in Norwich, Connecticut, a $35 note against a man in Massachusetts; saws, lathes, grindstone; bills of notes receipted by Brainard and Peck, charged Ingraham and Ross and one due Ingraham and Peck all the foregoing totaling $5,834.50; factory, land, lots, dwelling house and lot totaling $4,200. His appraised assets totaled $13,472.71.

Elias' accounts receivable from various customers in South Carolina and other southern states were not con-

Bankruptcy! 111

sidered of enough value to list. Chauncey Ives held most of the notes from Elias. There were eleven other holders listing notes ranging from $50 to $500 and 22 other creditors.

Total claims presented and allowed were $13,057. The only claim not allowed was "Balance of Elias Ingraham subscription for the benefit of the Methodist Church presented by Leander Hungerford for $5 . . . ." (Were the commissioners all Congregationalists?)

Thus it was that in the third year of the national depression Elias was bankrupt, losing his business and inventory, his home and land. His assets exceeded his liabilities by $415.71 which he assigned to Andrew. On February 14, 1842, Elias signed his name to a court document indicating liabilities as of that date in the amount of $15,389, owing 38 creditors including his brother-in-law, Chauncey Sparks of Glastonbury for $169.

Final disposition of his bankruptcy occurred March 25, 1845, when an undisbursed $33.72 was distributed, $9.33 to the court, $24.39 to other creditors "being 3 cents on the dollar."

At thirty-five, having been successful for a time, he found himself penniless, with little to show for thirteen years of work but considerable experience, developed talent and a sound reputation. In this bitter-sweet plight he was not alone. Most Bristol clockmakers were in the same sinking ship.

On January 16, 1840, the commissioners approved an agreement signed by Hopkins, Stevens and Chauncey Ives witnessed by Andrew Ingraham to settle Stevens' "claim against Elias Ingraham's assets for a sufficient number of Hayes Pat. easy chairs to cancel all my claim."

Some of the bills presented to the Court of Probate in connection with Elias' bankruptcy record:

To pay appraisers and commmissioners' bills, $12.75. To pay for lamp oil, firewood, account books and Lawyers' fee for advice, $5.05. To pay C. Sparks, A. Lane, O. Cook, A. Ingraham, and S. P. Burwell for work on chairs to fit for sale, $203.05. Probate fees, $28.00 To 29 days spent in said business as trustee, $45.50.

The item of $203.05 for about 162 hours' work to make unfinished chairs "fit for sale" tells mutely of Elias' inventory of uncompleted chairs which was salvaged for sale by Andrew and four helpers.

For $4,200 on April 9, 1840, faithful Andrew Ingraham from the trustee bought Elias' house, lot and buildings on West Street, and all the factory property, buildings, machinery and water rights. Thus Elias, Julia and ruddy little Edward were spared the loss of their home by the benevolent and modestly affluent Andrew and Rhoda Ingraham.

In 1837 Elias had countersigned Andrew's house mortgage. Now in 1840 the tide turned. Elias was unable to save his property. He faced eviction from factory and home. With innate generosity, Andrew stayed some of the relentless lashing. Indeed he saved the Elias Ingrahams from utterly losing their home.

Did he have faith that his investment in Elias would yet return? He found that for every nickel put into Elias there would come a tune, a cadence of a thousand times a thousand striking clocks!

On March 18, 1840, Andrew's account book enters "to Amount of Notes in favor of S. Talcott $3,145.76." This was an obligation of Elias which Andrew assumed. Elias' previous borrowings from Andrew and Rhoda added to the Talcott note brought Elias' debt to Andrew and wife to the sum of $4,237, exclusive of Elias' home. Among

Bankruptcy! 113

Elias' creditors was one Rhoda Ingraham, Andrew's wife who for some years had loaned him money.

On April 26, 1839, this entry appears in Andrew's account book, "the amount of Notes held against You at the time of your lienment $700.37." This was a summary of borrowings by Elias from Andrew and Rhoda. Before 1840 Elias returned her a total of $285.50. Apparently the second Mrs. Andrew Ingraham was a woman of means as well as of trust.

Elias' obligations to Andrew plus accumulated interest by 1849 had come to the prodigious sum of $7,534.32. By March 18, 1849, Andrew's account books showed that Elias had retired his total indebtedness to Andrew by payments in cash or in property to a remainder of but $2,459.22. Andrew's investment in his brother proved to be sound. Elias finally settled his obligations from profits of the then prospering firm of Brewster and Ingrahams but it had been a long ten years.

Taken by William A. Ives, the 1840 census records the Elias Ingraham household as composed only of ten-year-old Edward and his parents. There was no hired girl living in even though she might cost but a dollar or two a week. Things were tough indeed.

In the Andrew Ingraham household besides himself and Rhoda there were two women and a man between twenty and thirty.

The tax lists of October 1, 1840, show quite clearly the condition of these Ingraham brothers that unhappy year. Elias paid on only a cow plus a poll tax. Andrew paid on two houses, his and what had been Elias', six acres, manufacturies of $1,000 and a poll tax. Significantly, neither paid any occupation tax. They weren't gainfully occupied. In 1840 Andrew charged Elias for boarding Julia Darrow, Henry Stevens and Amasa Bronson. Both of these men were boarded until March of 1841. Why were these people boarded at all? We do not know. We can surmise, however, that this boarding was an extension of Elias' indebtedness to Andrew during Elias' financial extremity. Andrew and Rhoda were trying to make frayed ends meet.

Obviously to raise capital, on April 13, 1841, Andrew sold his own West Street house and lot bought in 1837. With Benjamin Ray he soon formed a partnership to make clocks. He needed capital. The two Ingraham families may have then lived under one roof for a time. If so, Elias may have yearned to get away from it all and thus been tempted to sail away as he did indeed.

After Elias' bankruptcy and before the Ray and Ingraham partnership, Andrew, typically energetic and resourceful, engaged a peddler to sell clocks and other articles. On September 23, 1840, Andrew and Timothy Abbe of Enfield, Connecticut, agreed that Abbe should peddle for Andrew for a period of fifteen months. Andrew furnished him with necessary horse, wagon and apparatus. Abbe's salary was $25 per month plus expenses. He agreed to bear the loss of all the bad debts which he might contract, to secure the materials to be sold, and to "devote himself faithfully and exclusively to the business of Andrew Ingraham," "to keep a true and just account of all his business transactions with his expenses" and to collect and remit monies due to Andrew.

Andrew otherwise busied himself in late 1840 and during 1841 towards reestablishing the clock business and in the reconstruction of his affairs.

On October 23, 1840, Andrew received from Elias in his own handwriting the following: "This may Certify that I Elias Ingraham do assign all my rite and title in a certain agreement betwixt myself and C & LC Ives dated Jan'y 11th 1840 to Andrew Ingraham." This assignment is the only known document over Elias' own signature

Bankruptcy! 115

between his bankruptcy and the 1843 partnership between Brewster and Ingrahams.

Adding to the cloud, Eunice Carrier Ingraham, mother of Elias and Andrew, died at Marlborough October 20, 1841, age 67. Her widowed husband, Joseph Ingraham III lived 17 years more. He married Lucy Bishop of Hebron on August 31, 1845. He died in Bristol on June 8, 1858 at the age of 82. Doubtless Andrew attended the funeral of his mother and Elias did also, if he were nearby.

The Andrew Ingraham affairs mended, gradually. On July 17, 1841, Andrew sold to Benjamin Ray for $1,175 a half interest in the North Main Street properties, factory, machinery and water rights formerly held by Elias. Ray and Ingraham formed a copartnership:

> . . . for the purpose of manufacturing clock cases or any other businefs they may mutually agree to embark in and in case one of the partis as an individual does furnish more capital than the other he is to be paid six per cent interest.
>
> The partis are to devote their time faithfully to the businefs of the Company and either of the partis shall not ingague in any indivudual businefs to interfere with the Company without the knowledg and concent of the other . . . The turm of this Copartnership shall contnue for the turm of four years or until mutually dissolved. At the dissolution of the Company the Establishment shall be sold to one of the parties concerned provided he will give as much as any other person and make as good pay. Each of the partis are to bear their Eaqual proportion of the Expense and Share eaqual in lofs and gain. The Sd Ingraham of the Second part is to have one dollar and thirty cents per day. In case the said Ingraham employs Elias Ingraham in the concern his time and service is to balance the Sd. Ray's service.

S. B. Jerome said that Benjamin Ray came from Vermont and entered the employ of Elias Ingraham in 1831. Ray was an excellent mechanic. His partnership with Carpenter known as Ray and Carpenter had recently burned out, dissolving the firm.

The mediocrity of Andrew as a craftsman was shown in his payment for his service at a twenty-cent lower daily rate than that of Ray. Though the partnership was scheduled for four years, it lasted but two or three since greener pastures for both Andrew and Ray lay ahead.

Elias was not a member of the firm of Ray & Ingraham although Andrew expected to employ him. After Elias' bankruptcy in 1840 he probably did some case work for Ray & Ingraham as well as for E. C. Brewster & Company.

Why was the hiring of Elias conjectural? Was he expected to be unavailable and off on a one-year's sailing voyage to Caracas? He may well have been since research and reason point to the 1842–1843 period as the most likely time for an absence.

For about two years Ray & Ingraham produced complete brass thirty-hour weight-driven pendulum clocks, commonly called "ogee." Clocks bearing the label "Ray & Ingraham" still exist. These are the earliest known clocks bearing the Ingraham name, albeit of Andrew, not Elias.

The assessment list of October 1, 1841, shows Elias Ingraham with a cow, a timepiece, poll tax and military tax, total taxes $41.02. This was quite a comedown and clearly expresses the plight of Elias at the first real low point of his business life. Andrew's assessment for the same year was one house at twelve hundred dollars (formerly Elias'), the same two and one-half acres at two hundred fifty dollars, one timepiece three dollars, poll tax, twenty dollars, occupational tax twenty dollars, total

Bankruptcy!

taxes paid, ninety-three dollars fifty-eight cents. Why Elias but not Andrew paid a military tax is unknown.

On July 26, 1841, Andrew credited himself and debited Ray and Ingraham for factory, machinery and veneers in the sum of $4,243.83. He also credited Ray and Ingraham $2,349.45 which probably was Ray's contribution to the partnership.

Between November 12, 1841, and June 14, 1844, Ray and Ingraham made and sold 10,044 clocks or clock cases. During 1843 and before June 14, 1844, the firm made 3,333 cases of the number two Gothic style, which was designed by Elias and called Round Gothic. Clock case sales were primarily to Chauncey Jerome, E. C. Brewster, Jerome and Grant, Chauncey Boardman, and E. Manross, all familiar names in Bristol's early clockmaking history.

Barter was still a widely used means of paying for clocks, especially in outlying areas. Yankee clock peddlers often were paid in barter items including cloth, carpeting, tub butter, feathers, potatoes, cedar shingles, fish, lumber, skins, "tinned" oil, farms, rags, harnesses, wagons, martingales, straw bonnets, bedsteads, cattle, horses. Payments were sometimes in hard money but more often in soft goods.

As the national depression lifted, by 1842 the ambitious Chauncey Jerome established a European market for American clocks. It expanded into 100 countries and even benefitted Ingrahams for generations to come.

Pursuant to the sale of clocks abroad, a contract between Chauncey Jerome and Epaphroditus Peck of Bristol was signed in November 1842. The agreement established Peck as European agent for the Jerome clock concern. Peck later represented the firm of Brewster and Ingrahams in the same foreign market. (This "Epaphroditus Peck died in London and was buried there. His place of burial was readily identified until destroyed by bombs in World War II. This Epaphroditus Peck was one of three Pecks to bear that name but the first two were never married and the last Epaphroditus left no son." —Edward Ingraham II)

Due to amazingly low manufacturing costs occasioned by mass production, American clocks undersold European clocks. South America became a good market for few if any clocks were made there. Did Elias develop that market as Jerome did the European? Clocks now became available worldwide, even to those of modest means.

After two or three years the Ray and Ingraham partnership was gradually dissolved. On May 1, 1844, Benjamin Ray for $1,400 sold his share of the firm of Ray and Ingraham back to Andrew. The inertia of the Ray and Ingraham factory gathered new momentum in the partnership of Brewster and the Ingrahams, formed the next year without Benjamin Ray.

On November 30, 1844, Ray sold to:

Elisha C. Brewster, Elias Ingraham and Andrew Ingraham under the firm name of Brewster and Ingraham for $5,000 the property located on the northeast corner of North Main and North St. [later known as "Eureka Shop"] together with the Factory and all other buildings belonging to the grantors and with all water privileges belonging to the premises and to include all shafts, belts, stoves and stove pipes, saw frames, handrill saws, benches, leveller and iron chest.

Elisha's ancestor, Elder William Brewster, came over on the Mayflower more than two centuries earlier. Brewster matched capital and acumen with the skills and experience of the brothers Ingraham. Brewster himself was a veteran clockmaker and business man. Between 1840 and 1843 his firm was known as Elisha C. Brewster and

Bankruptcy! 119

Company or Brewster and Ives, Shalor Ives having been his partner during a portion of that period. The new partnership of Brewster and Ingraham successfully operated for about a decade. The firm was a prolific producer of clocks. Many are extant to this day. The company operated in several plants in Bristol. They maintained a large clock export business.

> Report 1850, "Good, no doubt, Make 20 to 30,000 clocks annually and pay very well. Have real estate and buildings belonging to the Company, all clear . . . I fully believe they are to be trusted."
> (*The Book of American Clocks,* by Brooks Palmer)

Brewster was a professional clock manufacturer. He learned the trade traveling the South as a Yankee clock peddler for Thomas Barnes, Jr. and Company. He had earlier made cloth in Middletown, Connecticut. Brewster met Elias' need for a reinstatement in the clock business. Virtually penniless in 1843, Elias was heavily in debt to Andrew and would be for some years to come. Riches lay deep in his mind ready to surface anew from a fresh union of talent with opportunity. The clock bush was afire, not to be consumed. Astute men like the Ingrahams and Brewster would turn aside to see.

What in addition to everything else was the great talisman that Elias offered to so stir Elisha Brewster and Andrew Ingraham to abandon going concerns and to partner with him? Elias was broke but not broken when he returned from South America. The talisman he brought home was the magnificent Sharp Gothic clock design which was to become the most beautiful clock of his century. Besides, he may have found new markets in the Carribbean and South America.

The nation's growing industry in the East and its floods

of pioneers migrating west also cried out for clocks. Time was moving from sundials toward clock dials. The breezes of need blew afresh. Sky sails were hoisted, filling with winds of time tolled mechanically.

If Julia's head had been bowed through the bankruptcy, she now held it high. On September 3, 1843, about a month after Brewster and Ingrahams' founding, Julia joined the Bristol Congregational Society by profession of faith. This was ten years after her husband had joined. It was not uncommon for men in those days to join the church before their wives.

Elisha C. Brewster was, at fifty-two, fourteen years Elias' senior. Some say he was the first Connecticut clockmaker to mass produce clocks with American-made springs though Charles Kirk may have preceded him. Peter Henlein, a locksmith, of Nuremberg, Germany first used a coil spring as the motive power as early as the 16th century. So the idea was not new. Kirk sold his business in 1833 to Brewster and ran it for him for four years.

Clocks made by Brewster and Ingrahams containing brass springs were warranted not to fail. More than a century later many of these old clocks keep accurate time and are prized possessions among clock collectors. Strangely, the method used to temper the brass coil mainspring has been lost.

European clocks were not only expensive but difficult to repair. Wrote Charles Dickens:

> Since my hall clock was sent to your establishment to be cleaned it has gone (as indeed it always had) perfectly well, but has struck the hours with great reluctance, and after enduring internal agonies of a most distressing nature it has now ceased striking altogether. Though a happy release for the clock, this is not convenient for the household. If you can, send down any confidential person with

Bankruptcy! 121

whom the clock can confer. I think it may have something on its works that it would be glad to make a clean breast of.

The Bristol assessment records for October 1, 1844, show "Brewster and Ingrahams, two manufacturies 2250 dollars, occupational tax, two hundred dollars, total taxes paid two hundred sixty-seven dollars fifty cents." Already they were a substantial firm after but a year's operation.

From 1844 to 1849 the firm flourished. Their assessments for the period were four factories at $6,000, one store at $1,300, one horse at $65. The occupation tax varied from $100 to $125. Only one other Bristol firm during these years paid a larger occupation tax.

The period of Elias' life between his bankruptcy of 1840 and the Brewster and Ingraham clock company partnership of 1843 was one of adjustment, soul-searching, travel, transition. During this interim in his life, Elias may have taken the voyage to Caracas, Venezuela, a voyage fixed in family tradition by George Dudley Seymour, though otherwise undocumented by our ardent research in the archives of the United States and Venezuela.

One document from the Bristol *Press* handed down in the Ingraham family, upon which the Elias Ingraham trip to South America is founded, was written by Frederick Calvin Norton, more than three score years after the purported voyage. About 1930 George Dudley Seymour of New Haven told his nephew, Edward Ingraham II, that he supplied the facts used by Norton for the article. Seymour was a noted patent lawyer, antiquarian, as well as biographer of Nathan Hale.

Mr. Seymour (1859–1945) graduated from Columbia Law School and then opened a law office in New Haven for the practice of patent law. He was twenty-six when

Elias died, thirty-five when Julia Ingraham died. He knew them both. A confirmed bachelor, Seymour often came to Bristol to visit his three sisters, one of whom was the wife of Elias' grandson, William S. Ingraham. Here is the Seymour text reprinted in the Hartford *Daily Courant,* July 16, 1910, recognizing the twenty-fifth anniversary of Elias' death.

> Seeking a wider market for his clocks, Elias Ingraham went to Caracas, by sail, of course, and beguiled the tedium of the long return voyage by whittling out a design for a clock case from a block of wood, with his jack knife. This was the origin of the "Sharp Gothic" design, destined to play so large a part in the history of Yankee clocks.
>
> On his return to Bristol he made clock cases in accordance with this design and put them upon the market. They met with almost instant favor, and the design, under the trade-name "Sharp Gothic," became a favorite for small shelf-clocks. Had he protected the design by patent, he would have made a fortune, but as he failed to do that the design was copied by other makers and sold so extensively in this and foreign countries that it is believed to have been the "best seller" of any distinctively American design for clocks. Indeed, in remote parts, and particularly for export, this design still stands for reliability of performance and there is a steady demand for it. There seems to be no way of fixing the date of the voyage to Caracas, but I judge that it was in the "Roaring Forties" —earlier rather than later.
>
> To all this it may be well to add that the "Sharp Gothic" design as first produced in clock cases by Elias Ingraham was by far the best in point of design of any of the clock cases that ever received the name. His original design had a symmetrical peak or gable rising between two pairs of columns and two pairs of graceful pinnacles. This de-

sign as subsequently pirated frequently had only two columns and two pinnacles and a less symmetrical peak. As made today, the "Sharp Gothic" clock has little of the symmetry and style of Elias Ingraham's "Sharp Gothic," which is rarely met with. It may also be well to state that most of the popular designs for clock cases in use in the United States prior to 1875 were designed by Elias Ingraham, the most notable of these designs being the so-called "Grecian," "Doric," "Venetian," and "Ionic." All of these designs are standard designs in the foreign trade of American clock makers today.

The late Mr. Edward Stevens, for many years connected with The New Haven Clock Company, and for a long time its London representative, stated at a meeting of American clockmakers in New York that Elias Ingraham headed the list of all of the manufacturers of American clocks in the matter of designs. This statement was made by Mr. Stevens about 1879. Any unprejudiced critic today, on comparing Elias Ingraham's designs with the clock cases designed since his time and up to date, would readily give him the palm for superiority of design. The clock cases of the earlier days were as much superior in design to the clock cases of today as the furniture of the Colonial period was superior to the furniture of the "black walnut age."

Elias Ingraham was a man of heroic mould, tall, broad-shouldered, dignified and with a leonine head. Julia Sparks, his wife (of the Glastonbury family of that name), never forgave her husband for the leave he took of her when he went to South America. A high strung kind of woman, he seems to have dreaded breaking the news to her. One summer day he came home and astonished her by calling for his winter overcoat, which she gave him. He then left the house and the next she heard of him was from New York, where he wrote her a letter saying that he was sailing for South America. She re-

hearsed the story as long as she lived, but she never told it without a recurrence of her old feeling of resentment.
George Dudley Seymour
New Haven, Connecticut
June 1910

Elias Ingraham's "Sharp Gothic" clock design made him famous and finally rich, albeit the circumstances surrounding its origin were unforgiveable to his high-strung wife, Julia.

11

Art Surrenders to Disciplined Hands

1843

Architecture in general is frozen music.
—Friedrich Von Schelling

    Each generation inherits a digest of the design of the ages. Such a summary was Elias Ingraham's heritage. Conceptual patterns from his own pen and knife became petrified substance. In the reservoir of Elias' nature were treasures about to surface. These treasures doubtless were influenced by his study of architecture and art from which he discerned general principles of form and function.
    Out of this cadence came his creation, the Sharp Gothic, as two or three years earlier had come his invention of the Round Gothic.
    Dating of Gothic designs in shelf clocks has been until now conjectural, as still is the date of the famous Ingraham trip to Caracas. Andrew's account book first mentioned the Round Gothic in April, 1841, three or four months before the firm of Ray and Ingraham was formed and while Andrew was a free lance peddler. After bank-

ruptcy Elias designed the Round Gothic. Perhaps Andrew was first to sell it.

When Brewster and Ingrahams were still in their first year of business, Andrew's initial reference to the Sharp Gothic was in a sale in June 1844 to Myer, Geller and Fernald, probably clock wholesalers. Thus we reason that the famous purported trip to Caracas must have been completed by the summer of 1843. If Elias left in the summer and was gone a year, he may well have sailed to South America during the summer of 1842, returning with the Sharp Gothic prototype in mid-1843. Elias would thus have a year in Bristol to perfect the Gothic clock and interest his brother and Brewster in a partnership. Certain wording of the mid-1841 contract between Benjamin Ray and Andrew Ingraham leaves the feeling that Elias was not around to work in the firm, though he was expected to be available some time thereafter. Likely he was in the Caribbean.

The handsome Sharp Gothic, or Steeple clock, had classic proportions. It was gracefully pillared with two or four columns, topped with small finials set just above. This Steeple Clock indeed exhibited the artistic grace of the design-sensitive Ingraham nature.

A glimpse at the history of art which guided Elias may yield perspective on influences which instructed his head and hand.

After the War of 1812, the Greek style prevailed in both house and furniture, especially revivifying in England by the 1820s. Elias' apprenticeship and the first decade of his business life spanned periods of Greek and Gothic revivals.

American taste in art emerged in the 1830s. Aesthetic demands had not only to be met but created. The national slide from tastelessness to tastefulness was gradual but

Art Surrenders to Disciplined Hands

determined. Elias Ingraham was among the tastemakers of young America.

Cocksure Americanism placed Andrew Jackson in the White House for eight years in 1828. The age commenced not only of the common man but also of public taste. This phenomenon developed among both aristocrats and commoners, though some puckering occurred in their collective mouths. The newly rich demanded more tasteful surroundings and accessories.

Before the 1830s the tide of utilitarianism had been hard set against art. The functional was retained and improved but to it was added grace and style.

Mass production emerged as style developed, a fact demanding fresh attention by entrepreneurs like Elias Ingraham. As wealth increased, more and more people bought clocks, carpets, curtains, wallpaper and like amenities.

The Greek revival was the vogue through the 1830s. Into affluent homes went horsehair sofas, gilt mirrors, black backgrounded portraits, bright flowered carpets. Culture and commerce converged towards an early betrothal.

The history of art records a succession of revivals. In 1842 Andrew Jackson Downing of New York published *Cottage Residences*. This work was widely read and accelerated the development of taste in America. It laid the groundwork for Gothic architecture, replacing the waning Greek style.

Elias Ingraham returned from South America about the time that Downing's book was published, though we know of no Downing-Ingraham collaboration. They were independent subscribers to the reinstatement of the Gothic. Both were creative, stimulated by the same artistic climate. Ethnologists call this phenomenon "parallelism"—

"the independent development of similar elements or traits in several cultures from a common element."

Need and its fulfillment are often simultaneous. Flax may not be lacking to the ready spinning wheel. When primed and oiled the distaff becomes a point of the merging of the raw with the sophisticated, the finished cloth. Elias Ingraham in his clock designing became a ready spinning wheel primed by need and oiled by inspiration.

He developed a series of clock case creations involving rarity of idea with taste sophistication. The resultant creations were influenced by a composite of Egyptian, Grecian, Roman, Gothic, Georgian, and Colonial styles.

Underpinnings of ancient Egyptian furniture were carved to resemble bending human forms, symbols of subjection in which the Egyptians held their slaves and captives. As emblems of strength and power, the legs of their furniture ended in hooves of oxen, the talons of hawks or the paws of lions. Elias' lion's paw creation for George Mitchell's clock in 1827 had its genesis in Egyptian antiquity.

Later Greek furniture reflected the ideal of fine and beautiful proportions. It was slender and graceful, often decorated with glass, metal or ivory inlay. The Greeks mastered carved frets and scrolls. Pillar and Scroll clock styles found their antecedents in such Greek antiquity.

Egyptians and Greeks spent most of their talent on temples, tombs and public buildings. Archaic Romans were the first to surround themselves with beauty and comfort in their homes. Roman furniture was shaped much like that of the Greeks, but ornaments were added. It was painted and gilded. They developed what is believed to be the first form of wood-veneering. Elias Ingraham and other 19th century Yankee clockmakers used wood veneers in their clock cases, an idea reaching back to an ancient Romanic innovation.

Art Surrenders to Disciplined Hands

Conceived centuries before the Christian era, monumental classic styles, the Roman and Greek, were replete with columned porticos and domed interiors. The slender columns and graceful, tapering lines of some of Elias' clock styles originated from the ancient classical. Most creations of clock cases in 19th century use refer to two original styles of which they are modifications, to the classical where horizontal lines prevail, and to the Gothic where vertical lines predominate.

During the 700 years of the so-called dark ages in Europe, only two new styles developed: Byzantine and Romanesque. Huge and awkward, Byzantine furniture (mostly in oak and acacia) was inlaid and heavily carved with religious characters. The Romanesque was also heavily carved with figures of humans and animals. The human figures usually were in an attitude of bending in worship or slavery, recalling the ancient Egyptian style. Elias Ingraham and others frequently used carvings in their design reminiscent of these styles developed before the Renaissance.

The Gothic style appeared in France, spreading through Western Europe during the Renaissance in the twelfth to the fifteenth centuries. This was a period of religious and intellectual zeal. The idea of home as an important part of society was established during this period of intellectual flowering. Changing and promoting ecclesiastical art, the Gothic was an expression of majesty through verticality. Gothic principles carried over into building and decorating of houses and furniture. This style was appropriated and extended by clock case designers of the 17th, 18th and 19th centuries. The growing prevalence of Gothic as revived in the 1830s and 1840s captured the imagination of Elias, sensitive to beauty in style and trend. However, some Gothic style clocks existed in England prior to Elias' conception of a steeple clock.

The Georgian fathered the Colonial. In the 18th century Georgian architecture was of stone, Colonial of wood. The Colonial is a careful blending of delicate proportions. Cornices, moldings and ornamentations were fashioned more delicately in wood than in stone. The difference in materials used resulted in Colonial opportunities to change some of the classic proportions and execute buildings in more delicate dimension. This successfully changed classic proportions to a new conception of design —the Colonial, the first truly American style.

Mahogany was so commonly used in fine case work in the 19th century as to justify a word about it, especially in the light of speculation that Elias may have sailed the Caribbean in search of the source of mahogany and other fine woods.

For 50 years or more, mahogany had been used in fine furniture. The name in its present form developed in Jamaica. The word originated during the period of revolution between 1655 and 1670. Mahogany has had a linguistic evolution from an African origin with Portuguese and English amendments. A native Jamaican tree produced excellent wood for ship construction and repairs. A local term for this tree was "mogano" as used by Portugese settlers and African slaves. Tribes of Southern Nigeria comprised a considerable portion of the slaves imported to Jamaica; these slaves furnished the word's root from their nomenclature for their homeland's forest trees. Their tribal language traces the similar term as used for a tree now known as African mahogany. The root of the term means "to be tall, high, distinguished and glorious." And so it was as Elias sought "mogano" trees of the Caribbean.

Art Surrenders to Disciplined Hands

From a block of this self-same Caribbean "mogano," Elias carved the first model of the Sharp Gothic clock.

Remember, O Elias, remember your apprentice days in Glastonbury! Recall the words of your master. Can you still hear him say, "The music hidden in the violin is frozen until the coaxing bow in the hand of the skilled artist draws forth the melted melody?" Do you hear his voice echoing down the long dusty corridor of time, "Within the rough marble lies the hidden David, the Pieta, which the sensitive hands of Michelangelo discovered through patient chiseling?" Listen again to those words of long ago, "The frozen song, the unyielding marble must surrender their fruitage under the disciplined and compelling hands."

12

A Faithful Brother

1844-1854

Success in life is a matter not always so much of talent or opportunity as of concentration and perseverance.

—C. W. Wendte

The Farmington Canal was eventually abandoned. Early in 1846 a survey for a railroad on the towpath was conducted by the canal owners. "Green" Irish railroad workers boarded in Bristol for $1 per week, $1.25 if with coffee. The age and benefits of the iron horse were upon Connecticut clockmakers. The Hartford, Providence and Fishkill Railroad reached nearby Plainville in 1848, Bristol by 1850. White pine, mahogany, cherry, maple and rosewood soon arrived in Bristol by rail and finished clocks went out on "the cars."

Brewster and Ingrahams were large lumber users. Benjamin Ray supplied them with veneers after he removed to Bridgeport. Imported logs from foreign countries were put into vats of hot water after which veneers were cut or sliced for use in finished clock cases.

Brewster and Ingrahams were now in the midst of a roaring decade. Tens of thousands of clocks were moving

A Faithful Brother

out of Bristol from their factories. Elias brought out many successful case designs. No other case would excel the grace and beauty of his Sharp Gothic, likely the largest selling shelf clock design ever produced.

This verse has been found in at least one of the Ingraham clocks:

> I serve thee here with all my might
> To tell the time both day and night.
> Therefore example take from me
> And serve thy God as I serve thee!

Immigration from Europe began to increase greatly. Wave after wave of the European downtrodden surged onto America's shores. Elias Ingraham was at the dock in Castle Garden in New York City to meet one such German immigrant, Christian Funck. Elias needed qualified woodworkers to fashion clock cases. Among the thousands of German immigrants were many expert artisans. Funck and three other newcomers were induced by Ingraham to come to Bristol to work in the busy clock shops.

Later in business for himself, Funck by 1871 advertised his black walnut furniture in the first issue of the Bristol *Press*. He and his son, Augustus, were simultaneously engaged in furniture making and undertaking. Their firm which was founded in 1865, still in business a hundred years later, served as undertakers for many Ingrahams, including Elias and Andrew, Julia and Edward I.

Epaphroditus Peck met with good success in selling Brewster & Ingrahams' clocks in Europe. He was retained as their agent into the early 1850's. Elisha Brewster's son, Noah, also represented the firm in London beginning in 1844. In 1852, brash Noah precipitated the dissolution of Brewster and Ingrahams.

On April 23, 1845, some boys playing with matches

at the rear of the Bristol Jerome factories set afire some shavings under the floor. They ignited the most disastrous fire that ever occurred in Bristol to that time. Clock shops, storage and lumber sheds, stables, with costly clock making machinery including a clock inventory valued at $50,000 or more, went up in flames. $10,000 of fire insurance covered but a fraction of the loss.

After the fire, sick in bed with typhus fever, Jerome philosophically wrote of his feelings:

> It was hard indeed to grapple with so much in one year, but I tried to make the best of it and to feel that these trials, troubles and disappointments sent upon us in this world, are blessings in disguise.

Ten years later Elias Ingraham would himself know similar trials, troubles and disappointments when his clock factory would also burn to the ground.

In the mid-eighteen hundreds many United States merchants carried substantial balances with South American firms. Daniel Pratt, Jr., 1797–1871, of Reading, Massachusetts, received coffee among other things as payment for clocks. From Brewster and Ingrahams he purchased movements which he shipped by water in spring and summer, over land by team when the Connecticut River was frozen. Augustine Wills and Company, agents for Pratt, sold for him hundreds of brass and wooden movements in Calcutta. Thus it was that Brewster and Ingrahams' clock movements reached India, at least under a Daniel Pratt, Jr., label.

Enterprising Fredrick Tudor of Boston pioneered the shipping of ice in the holds of sailing vessels destined for warm climates. In 1806 he shipped ice to the West Indies, in 1833 to Calcutta. By 1856 Boston was shipping abroad the incredible total of 146,000 tons of ice annually. Clocks transported in such sailing ship holds were carefully

A Faithful Brother

packed indeed. During the "roaring forties" return cargoes for payment included indigo, raw silk, gunney cloth, black dye, and saltpeter.

Peer for a moment into the mind and heart of Andrew Ingraham as he faces the swift flow of years and prepares his will:

> In the Name of God Amen This 10th Day of Nov 1845 I Andrew Ingraham of Bristol . . . Being in a Disposing mind and memory make and ordane this my last Will and testment Viz In the first place I give and recommend my Soul to God who gave it and my body to the Earth to be deasentley Beery'd And as to such Worley Goods as it has pleased God to besto on me I'd Give and dispose of in the following manner Viz
>
> My Will is that my just Debts and Funeral Charges be justley and truley paid in Cluding Six Hundred Dollars which I justley Owe to My Well be Loved Wife Rhoaday Ingraham it being Money which she Urned be fore And Brought with her When I Married her Which I have received and used, to be paid by my Executors Here in after named. I Give to My Brother Elias Ingraham My Factory and Water Privolege in Cluding the Land which I own Connectid with the Faitory Lying East of the High Way running past it with all Bildings there on Standing, And all the Masheanry in the Factory Provided he pay or Caus to be paid to Samuel Talcott Seventeen Hundead Dollars the pris'd Valieu of the Property when I bought it And Two Hundread Dollars with the Interest which I Owe to Chauncey Ives, And Pay to my Well be Lovid Wife Rhody Ingraham Five Hundread Dollars Or if the Said Samuel Talcott & Chauncey Ives have received there pay He then Pay the Same amount to my Well be Lovid Wife Rhody Ingraham.
>
> Furthermore I Give to My Wife Rhody the care and Improvemente of all My Real and Personal Estate Except what I have Given to My Brother Elias Solong as she remains my Widow And all my Houshold Furniture

forever to her one Disposal If there Should be any thing remaning of my Real on Pursonal Estate after the Decese of my Wife my Will iz that it be Devidid Equaley to the American Bible Society & the Forren and Home Misheon Societies And I hereby nominate and appoint My Well be Lovid Wife Rhody Ingraham And Brother Elias Ingraham Exectors . . . .

Andrew Ingraham

Hopkins Stevens
Richard H. Stevens

This will was not Andrew's last, for he outlived both Rhoda and Elias. It is here reproduced for its insight into Andrew's affairs and solid character in the mid-1840s.

Andrew's forty-page account book has entries between 1846 and 1852 that reveal some workings of the clock company. He records purchase of black walnut crotches at 12½¢ each, from W. and D. Humphries in Ohio, 50,000 feet of walnut at $18.50 per thousand. Payment was to be made in clocks. He records clock orders, mostly Gothic, shipped in boxes to the west. He listed an inventory of thousands of clocks and components in various stages of completion, including Sharp and Round Gothic, OG, Looking Glass, Marine and Gilt.

Andrew's account book, between May 26th and Dec. 1852 has this significant notation: "Mr. Elias Ingraham 13 Walbrook City, London, England by steamer." The address was that of the London sales office of Brewster and Ingrahams. Did Elias go to Europe by steamer in 1852? Did he there become disenchanted with Elisha Brewster's obtrusive son, Noah, whom he reckoned to be inadequately representing Brewster and Ingrahams? The dissolution of the co-partnership between Brewster and the Ingrahams was a painful experience disrupting and terminating a near-decade of a prosperous enterprise.

These quotations from his account book reveal Andrew's distress at the time:

A Faithful Brother   137

But as Milton once said to his favorite daughter, It matters little whether one has a star to guide or angel hand to lead; and Lizzy, we must learn to bear and blaim not that which we cannot change.

The journey of life is short. We may not stop here long, and sorrow and trial discipline the spirit, and educate the sole for a future life; and those upon whom we most depend, we love most.

As gold was discovered in distant California a contract involving gold in the form of clocks for the firm of Brewster and Ingrahams was made with Anson L. Atwood (1816–1906). Atwood was a skilled mechanic making clock parts by contract. Happily a copy of this contract has been preserved:

> . . . witnesseth, that the said Atwood, on the first part, agrees to make, within the space of one year from the above date, twelve thousand brass eight day spring clock movements, for the sum of thirty-one cents for each movement, after the plan of these made by Pomeroy & Robbins in 1847, it being understood that he is to convert so many of the above twelve thousand movements as the said Brewster & Ingrahams may desire, into thirty hour movements, by shortening the springs. The said Atwood also agrees to make, within the same time as above, five thousand timepiece movements, for the sum of twenty-five cents for each movement, and four thousand five hundred timepiece movements, for the sum of eighteen cents for each movement, after the plan of those made by Pomeroy & Robbins in 1847 . . . .
>
> The said Atwood is to finish the movements as fast as the said Brewster & Ingrahams shall need them, and on the delivery of every one thousand movements he shall be entitled to receive one half of the sum stipulated for making one thousand movements, the other half of said stipulated sum is to remain unpaid until the foregoing

contract shall have been completed. In witness whereof we hereunto set our hands this twenty-third day of March 1848.

Anson L. Atwood
Brewster & Ingrahams

Employees were provided with living quarters in the factory. Their duty was to open the shop in the morning and to make the fires. This was before the days of friction matches. Instead of a match they used a round file which was held against a piece of iron wire until red hot. A brimstone match was then put against it. In cold weather the water wheel was frozen solid. It was necessary then to go under the shop in the dark and chop the wheel loose from the ice, a task disenchanting to one just out of a warm bed.

As tens of thousands of hardy fortune seekers rushed to California with gold fever, Andrew Ingraham made a six weeks' business trip to the midwest for his clock firm. His mission was to sell clocks, collect bills, and appraise credit.

He recorded his trek with a steel pen in a small rag-paper diary now a treasure in the American Clock Museum in Bristol. His rural spelling is delightful.

On June 17, 1849, Andrew left Cleveland for Parma, Ohio in a clattering horse-drawn stage. He writes that he arrived "much coverid with dust."

Walking the last two and one half miles to Woodville, Ohio, Andrew visited his father's younger brother, Benjamin Ingraham. He "Partid with Uncle and Aunt together with his children and children's children. Bidding them fare well never expecting to see them any more."

His visit smacked of enterprise for his account book records an order from one of his cousins for twelve 30-hour Gothic clocks.

On July 2 Andrew stepped aboard a line boat on the

"Morme Canall." He saw the Morme Indian Missionary Station. Only six years before, the Wyandotte Indians had been evicted from Ohio and compelled to move to Indian Territory to the West. Passing through locks into the muddy Marme River, the boat stopped for one hour while the tow-line horses were shod.

On July 4 Andrew wrote:

> Arivd in Ft. Wayne about 8 OC A.M. Found there was no stage that was to go to Gotion [Goshen, Indiana] untill Fyrday morning but on looking around found a team that was going on towards Gotion that would take me along with them and so I put aboard about 10 oclock and startid on towards Gotion passing threw a very productive section of cuntry and over a verry rough logway roade ariving at Wolfe Lake about 7½ OC P.M.

There he accepted an invitation to march in the temperance procession with 75 or 100 "gentlemen & lades . . . with a band of music composed of one base & snare drum and clarronett when we marchid to the place of meting and there listionid to an adress from a gentleman for sum 10 or 15 minuits. And then were invitid to protake of sum refreshments which had bin provided with a grate expense, for one shilling a peese the ladis having the prefferance of course and after that if there was roome the gentlemen sat down. But as I thought there mite not be roome for all and my Landlord was expecting me back to tea with him I did not stop to pertake."

The next morning Andrew left in a private conveyance with a man who was taking a drove of horses to Michigan. Laconically he wrote of that day:

> Passing threw sum shours and dry wether sumtimes wet and sumtimes coverd with dust, I cleaned up sum and then went out and saw T. G. Harris [lawyer and later

state senator] and found that the money had bin sent on to Bristol, so I preparid muself for starting on again.

On Sunday July 8, Andrew arrived at Detroit too late for church but in time for a Sunday School evening concert and a young men's well attended and interesting prayer meeting:

> Where I found myself at home in a place where I could be freed from the nois and commotion of this world and could unite with those that were seeking a happer and bettor world.

He took a Lake Erie boat to Buffalo arriving there sixteen hours later where he "Brakefirst at Bennet's Temperance House . . ." From a horse car he viewed with awe the suspension bridge built the year before over the whirlpools below Niagara Falls. He called the bridge a "greate artificial peace of work."

Going on to Kingston, Ontario via horse and steam car and steamboat, he was joyfully impressed with his travels as he wrote,

> What differente locations the traveler finds himself in. Yesterday I was sailling acrost the waters of Lake Eary. 10 days I have bin traviling on land and vewing the works of nature and arte and now find myself sum 250 ft. or 300 ft. below the waters of Lake Eary swimming along like a bird acrost the waters of Lake Ontario, clear and pure as the waters of the vast otion. Retired to rest after having a sotiable chat with John Eberly, a gentleman with whome I became acquainted with the winter that I spent in Pensilvany.

Later at Brockville he uncomplainingly wrote,

> Retired to rest on a bead of straw, rather hard, yet the night being hot I got along with it verry wall.

A Faithful Brother

On Sunday, July 15, Andrew attended the Oswego, New York Presbyterian Church. The sermon was apropos of Andrew's business mission:

> Owe no man anything but to love one another, giving us a thurrow practical discourse setting forth the importance of a Cristian paying promptly at the time agread and the withholding of money from another after it became due when we had the means to pay was nothing less than putting our hands into his Jinns and taking from him his property. It was robbery. It was using his and not our owne money and that the world would judge of us according to the transactions of our bisness with them and not according to our position.

Traveling through dust and mud Andrew wrote of the problem of keeping his clothes clean as mentioned in his entry for July 19,

> . . . concludid that it was not possible for to get home this week and as it would be nesisary for me to have sum washing dun in ordor to have a change, I concludid to stop over till Friday.

After completing his business at Albany on July 23, he wrote:

> Then starting for the boat arrivid at the Whoff just in time to jump aboard of the Hendric Hudson and took passage for New York.

Twenty-two hours later he docked at New York City and soon was home again in Bristol. His diary concludes with:

> Found my famaley and friends all wall and was thankfull to return again to my famaley after being so long absent from them.

Andrew traveled 2,800 miles in 40 days, passed through five states in two nations, afoot, by horse and steam cars, by buggy, wagon, private conveyance, stage coach, line and steam boats and packet. He not only traveled but travailed.

In 1851 Brewster and Ingrahams, along with other clock makers, placed advertisements in the Connecticut Business Directory. Among the advertisers was The American Clock Company, Cortland Street, New York City. They invited prospective customers to view at their "depot" over one hundred thousand dollars' worth of clocks from at least eight prominent clockmakers, including Brewster and Ingrahams.
The ad read:
"Orders from any part of the United States, Canada, West Indies, Mexico, or Europe promptly attended to."
On page 143 is a page taken from that 1851 Directory.
Just before Andrew returned from his western business trip in 1849 Brewster and Ingrahams and eight associates bought five acres including factory shop, sheds and other buildings with water privileges together with machinery and tools used for clockmaking for $6,500. Within a few years all the eight men had sold back their shares to the firm or its partners.
Elias was prospering. In 1850 he involved himself in the Bristol Knitting Mills and in Bristol Brass Company's formation. He was among its sixteen founders. The company made brass springs for Bristol's 50 clockmakers and showed a $60,000 profit in two years!

The fortunes and misfortunes of Elias were clearly visible in Bristol records of assessments. In 1841 he was taxed for one cow and a clock or watch. That was all. For the next eight years he was personally taxed for

A Faithful Brother 143

nothing more. By 1850 his affairs had improved. He then owned a house and a fifty-dollar piano. This property evaporated from his ownership in 1856. We shall see why.

BREWSTER & INGRAHAMS
Have constantly on hand, at their factory, in
BRISTOL, CONN.,
Their various Styles of Patent Spring Eight Day and Thirty Hour
BRASS CLOCKS,
In Mahogany, Zebra, Rosewood and Black-Walnut Cases.

Also Gallery, Hall and Counting-House Eight Day Time-Pieces of 10 inches to 22 inches in diameter, in Gilt, Mahogany and Black

WALNUT CASES

Also an Improved Kind Of Eight Day and Thirty Hour
MARINE TIME-PIECES,
All which are made in the best manner.

* * *

The Proprietors are constantly present to attend to all orders, whether large or small, at as low prices, regard being had to quality, as at any other Factory in the country.

They Have Also A House At

No. 13 WALBROOK, CITY LONDON, ENGLAND

Where they keep constantly on hand a large assortment of the above kinds of Clocks, together with Eight Day and Thirty Hour
OG WEIGHT CLOCKS
Please call and examine before purchasing elsewhere.

E. C. Brewster   E. Ingraham   A. Ingraham

Andrew's affairs were less volatile than his brother's. Besides, his wife was a woman of modest means and certain generosity. In 1841 Andrew had a twelve hundred dollar house, two and one half acres, a five dollar clock or watch. This property continued to be his major personal holdings until 1854 when he added about fifteen acres with cattle.

The growth of the co-partnership between the Ingraham brothers and Deacon Brewster is also recorded in the city archives. The company started in 1843 with two factories valued at $2,250. The next year they added a third factory and a horse. By 1846 they owned four factories valued at $6,000. By 1851 the firm reached its peak with six factories assessed at $15,000. That year they paid the prodigious sum of $918 in taxes. The next year, their terminal one, the assessment dropped to $10,000.

Elisha Brewster, during this period, was a man of some means. In 1850 he owned a house; fourteen acres; one each of a cow, sheep and swine; farming utensils; mechanical tools; hay; grain; farm products; furniture; libraries and musical instruments valued at $475 and manufactures and stocks valued at $1,334. At 59, Brewster was passing his prime and within a few years retired, although he lived to be eighty-nine.

Having not owned a home for ten years, on April 17, 1850, from C. E. Smith, Elias bought a three-year-old $1,500 house just south of Andrew's property on West Street. The assessment included furniture, library, and musical instruments valued at $300. He and Julia owned this house until bought in 1856 by Hammond Beach who, in 1861, resold it to his daughter, Eliza Jane, then Mrs. Edward Ingraham I.

Clear evidence of dissension in the Brewster and Ingrahams partnership appeared on April 17, 1852, when Elias and Andrew sold their interests in a portion of company properties back to Elisha Brewster. About three months later Andrew sold to Elias half interest in the North Main Street property, buildings and water rights

A Faithful Brother 145

which, while a part of operation for Brewster and Ingrahams, had never been owned by Brewster.

Disassociation appeared on July 24, 1852, when Elias and Andrew began significant independent operations calling their firm E. and A. Ingraham. Formal dissolution of Brewster and Ingrahams occurred at the end of 1852, although two more years were required for a complete settlement.

Dudley S. Ingraham, of Litchfield, Connecticut, younger son of William S. Ingraham, says: "I had it both from Father and Epaphroditus Peck that a break was created between Brewster and Ingrahams because Brewster insisted on having his son represent the firm in England where he succeeded Epaphroditus Peck who had developed a fine English business for Brewster and Ingrahams. Young Brewster was an absolute failure and apparently the Ingrahams insisted on a change in the set up."

On the fourth Tuesday of January, 1853, a petition by Elisha Brewster to the superior court in Hartford was filed indicating his dissatisfaction with the Ingraham brothers regarding the dissolution of the firm. Brewster complained that the Ingrahams were tardy about coming to a fair and final settlement and that the Ingrahams "neglected and refused so to do and still do neglect and refuse so to do and that he [Brewster] is unable to procure a just, fair and resonable account from and with the defts. [defendents] of their partnership business and accounts."

The sheriff of Hartford county, through the Bristol constable, was commanded to summon both Elias and Andrew to appear before the court to show reason why "the prayer of the foregoing petition should not be granted." Alphonso Warner, deputy sheriff, served the summons.

The dispute was resolved out of court. On the back of the document is written "withdrawn." Apparently the case was dismissed, and satisfaction was obtained by Elisha Brewster although the complexity of their joint affairs required a long period of disengagement. The break marked the end of nearly a decade of prosperous association by three stalwart clockmakers who together left an indelible mark for generations to come in the history of mid-nineteenth century clockmaking in Bristol.

In 1850 Bristol's population was 2,284 souls. Clockmakers in the United States totaled 1,436. Of these, 837 were in Connecticut, about sixty percent. Bristol's clock production was 200,000 annually.

In September, 1850, twenty-year-old Edward Ingraham I entered the freshman class at Yale University law school. Cheerful and personable, he exhibited the spirit of a typical college youth. Like many another collegian before and since, Edward was counselled to conduct himself with discretion. From the original in his own good hand, here is the only letter extant from his college days, written to an uncle, in all probability his dear Uncle Andrew Ingraham:

"Yale College"
Feb. 2d/1852

Dear Uncle.

Your very kind letter of the 26th inst. was duly and gratefully received. Although I am blessed with many uncles and aunts, with whom I have ever been on the best of relations, I have never yet borne toward them the relation of a correspondent. Your letter was therefore gladly received on this account. I have ever considered that the next thing to being with one's friends, is a mental reunion through the medium of letters—and that if correspondence was more of the nature it should be and more faithfully pursued, friends would be better friends, and relations more firmly linked together.

Feeling grateful at the marks of consideration and interest exhibited in your letter I hasten to reply. Your

A Faithful Brother

affectionate counsel was . . . fully received and read with careful consideration. The imperious necessity of improving what advantages may in earlier years be offered us is, to every thinking mind, very obvious—youth is the sowing time of life,—manhood and age reap the fruits, if good seed is carefully and faithfully sown—then shall the full ear and heavy grain, repay the labor; but if, the spring time be idled away in the sunshine of profitless pleasure, the winter shall find the garner empty—and remorse and unavailing regret be added to want.

Such were the thoughts called forth by your words of advice, and again I thank you for them. In almost constant association with more than half an hundred young men of nearly my own age, I could, perhaps, have no better opportunity for the Observation of character and disposition, than is thus prevented. It is an easy matter to predict who from among the number will be the eminent and respected *men*. It will not be those who are frittering away the best days of their lives, either in positive indolence, or employed in pursuits to which indolence is preferable; but it will be those, who are patiently and perseveringly preparing themselves, who are, as it were, forging or burnishing their armor and weapons for the impending battle of life.

I received a letter this morning from father, from which I find that he and mother are at home again. I have not, as yet, had an opportunity of calling upon Mr. Goodrich, but will do so if possible. There is no news here at present of interest. Give my love to aunt, and hoping to hear from you again I remain your affectionate nephew.

Edward Ingraham

That young Edward Ingraham may have been frittering away some time himself was made evident by his rustication from Yale. The circumstances surrounding his expulsion remain obscure. What is known, however, is that his friend and fellow law student, Edmund Clarence Stedman, was rusticated about the same time.

Stedman later wrote of himself at Yale as imaginative, excitable, reckless, unstudious, prone to cut prayers. He spent his nights with beer, whiskey-skin, skittles and "howling around town." At the end of his sophomore year he was arrested, taken before "dogberry" (a foolish constable in Shakespeare's Much Ado About Nothing). Reported to the faculty, Stedman was quickly dismissed. President Woolsey refused his re-entry. A few years later Stedman became a partner in the firm called Ingrahams and Stedman. Still later he was known as the "banker-poet" of Wall Street.

Edward Ingraham I journeyed to Milford from Yale to court Eliza Jane Beach. A choice bit of insight into this persistent foray has been handed down by a descendant of Eliza Jane who wrote:

> [Edward] . . . when a student at Yale used to come to Milford every week courting Pa's "Cousin Jane" and always went over to "the store" and told Mr. Bristol to "Set 'em up!" and "the boys" always looked forward to "Ingraham night."

The remnant of Puritanism in Elias and Julia Ingraham eroded in their somewhat thriftless collegiate son. Although reliable, Edward Ingraham I was all his life rather more improvident than either his father or Uncle Andrew.

Eliza Jane Beach (1834–1895) attended Emma Willard School. Many of her Milford ancestors distinguished themselves in Colonial times. Twenty-four-year-old Edward and twenty-year-old Eliza Jane were married by Rev. J. K. Brace on June 6, 1854. Edward then was working with his father and Uncle Andrew for the E. and A. Ingraham Clock Company, perpetuating the name Ingraham for generations to come.

13

The Purge of Fire

1852-1860

As in nature, as in art, so in grace; it is rough treatment that gives souls, as well as stones, their lustre.

—Guthrie

This set of rules, hung in 1854 as a guide to employees in what is today one of the world's leading department stores, provides a glimpse of both the austerity and the piety of the times:

THE FOLLOWING RULES
WILL BE PUT IN FORCE
AT ONCE:

Store must be opened promptly at 6 A.M. and remain open until 9 P.M. the year around.

Store must be swept: counters, base shelves and show cases dusted. Lamps trimmed, filled and chimneys cleaned; pens made; doors and windows opened; a pail of water, and a scuttle of coal must be brought in by each clerk, before breakfast if there is time to do so, and attend to customers who call.

Store must not be opened on the Sabbath Day unless absolutely necessary and then only for a very few minutes.

Any employe who is in the habit of smoking Spanish cigars, getting shaved at a barber shop, going to dances and other such places of amusement, will most surely give his employer reason to be suspicious of his integrity and all around honesty.

Each employe must pay not less than $5.00 per year to the church and must attend Sunday School every Sunday.

Men employes are given one evening a week for courting purposes, and two if they go to prayer meeting regularly.

After 15 hours of work in the store, the leisure time must be spent in reading good literature.
(From *Clockmakers of Bristol, Connecticut, 1937*, Lockwood Barr and Carlton W. Buell)

While factories making clocks had shorter hours than department stores, the age of employer-employee relations was still Calvinistic. There was little separation between church and store. Edward Ingraham I's generation was the first to break away from such rigid modes of conduct. They smoked cigars, were publicly shaved or bearded as they pleased.

The commercial manufacturer of American clocks had undergone a transition from tall to shelf in 1815, wooden to brass after 1838, weight-driven to spring wound about 1842. A typical mid-nineteenth century mechanical timepiece had four basic elements: a weight or spring sourcing the power; a gear train changing the motion of the power source to drive the hands; an escapement preventing the power from exhausting itself in one quick spin; and a dial or face recording the time.

In 1852 a $2,800 partnership between Elias and Andrew called E. and A. Ingraham commenced. Edward I

The Purge of Fire

was a partner in this firm by 1855 if not before. The partnership made clocks until bankrupted in 1857. Edward I began working for his father and uncle sometime following his preemptory invitation to leave Yale.

E. and A. Ingraham and several other contemporary clockmakers were no quantitative match for the Jerome Company. In 1853 Jerome at New Haven was the largest clockmaker in Connecticut, turning out nearly half a million clocks annually. His company failed in 1855, the year that a devastating fire struck the Ingrahams in Bristol. Petulant Chauncey Jerome died in 1868 in near poverty, broken in health and spirit. The Ingrahams would not only resuscitate but move on to success and prosperity, albeit not without continuing difficulties.

On July 7, 1855, Andrew sold half of his interest in the firm of E. and A. Ingraham to Edmund C. Stedman. Undoubtedly Edward Ingraham I persuaded his college chum and fellow rusticatee to enter the Ingraham firm.

Assuming charge of the branch store in New York called Ingrahams and Stedman, 48 Courtland Street, Stedman was more interested in writing than in selling clocks. The following spring after the disastrous fire of the Ingraham plants in Bristol, he resold his one-sixth interest back to Andrew. At its unfortunate dissolution in 1857 E. and A. Ingraham was owned one-sixth by Edward Ingraham I; one-third by Andrew and one-half by Elias.

Stedman's memoirs contribute to our awareness of Yale University life at the time Edward Ingraham I and he were undergraduates. A year ahead of Edward, precocious Stedman at 15 entered Yale law school in 1849. Virtually orphaned, never robust, he had rather long black hair, cut squarely, just above a turned-down collar. During his college days he boarded for $2.50 a week, bought firewood at $9 a cord. His freshman year at Yale cost $300.

He and Edward I rose at 6:30 A.M., ran to prayers and recitations before breakfast and after lunch, retired at 10:30 or 11:30 P.M. after studying. During his sophomore year Stedman lived in the fourth floor of the oldest college building which he described as having mouldy, crumbling walls, bare floors full of rat holes, through which the bitter wind whistled. Later, Stedman became a nationally known poet, critic and editor. He was the first war correspondent covering the Civil War for the *New York World* in 1861. Stedman's clock company contributions were minimal but we must add that his nine months' tenure in the Ingraham clock business, punctuated by a ruinous fire, was hardly a fair measure of the Stedman talent.

As a private enterprise, in 1853, Alphonso Barnes and Colonel E. L. Dunbar organized the first Bristol fire department, Hose Company number one. Jerome's egregious factory fire in 1845 emphasized the need of local, organized fire protection. Over $2,000 was raised, an engine house constructed, a hand engine and a horse-drawn wagon with 500 feet of hose purchased. The original company was comprised of sixty men, a number none too large for a hand-operated engine. When a fire started in a combustible wooden factory of that day, there was not much that could be done to stop it, even with an organized and willing fire department using "modern" hand pumps drawing water from nearby brooks or ponds.

Little short of spontaneously combustible, clock factories burned as the rule rather than the exception. Heating facilities were dangerous, stoves being of the pot-bellied type burning wood and shavings. Overturned whale oil lamps started many a conflagration. A leather

The Purge of Fire

bucket brigade was the earlier means of putting out fires until superseded by hand pumps.

A decade of one difficulty after another descended upon 50-year-old Elias. On a sharp, bitter-cold Thursday morning early in December, 1855, his leonine heart was again fearfully tried. A $20,000 fire burned his factory to the ground and ruined the intrepid clockmaker financially. This misfortune would be followed by the untimely breaking of a water wheel, by another national depression, by another bankruptcy in 1857, by the need to start all over again, by the oncoming four years of the Civil War which crippled and plagued the clock industry as well as the nation for generations to come.

Edward I's health reportedly broke under the strain and he moved to Chicago. Andrew gave up the clock business and moved to Guilford, Connecticut. Indomitable Elias, seasoned, courageous, redoubtable, energetic, had to start up a third time literally from the ashes of the fire.

The fire of 1855 was a cruel blow to E. and A. Ingraham as reflected in the October, 1856, Bristol assessment which showed an ownership of two acres, $1,500 valuation in factories, and $500 in miscellaneous, with zero in investments in trade.

As good as their word, the Ingrahams promptly removed their operations to a vacant clock factory at nearby Ansonia. There, by January, 1856, they made cases, bought movements from Pomeroy and Parker of Bristol, from the New Haven Clock Company and possibly from others. A few E. and A. Ingraham clocks marked "Ansonia" are extant to this day. The Ingrahams' stay in Ansonia was short-lived and agonizing.

About six weeks after the fire Edward I wrote to his Uncle Andrew Ingraham at Bristol an urgent letter:

Ansonia
Jan. 24th 1856

Mr. A. Ingraham

Dear Sir:

We yesterday wrote to Henry Beckwith in relation to that stove at Polkville for heating requesting him to send it immediately.

We've since thought it would be best to purchase some of the other things, viz: O.G. clocks the price named is $25.00. Large sand paper wheel $15.00 small ditto $8.00. Wish you would see to it and have them sent along with the stove as soon as possible and at as low rate as possible.

Yours Most Truly
E. and A. Ingraham & Co.

While Andrew was besought by his nephew in Bristol to expedite materials and tools, trouble brewed in icy Ansonia around their water wheel. Every clock factory in New England in the mid-19th century had its water wheel. Falling water was the source of power which ran factory machinery through a series of belts from the main axle. Protection against flood was achieved by ponding and fluming water to the wooden wheel-buckets. In winter the problem of ice continually threatened the operation of every such mechanism.

The big iron shaft of this breast wheel at the rented Ansonia plant became loaded with ice, broke down, critically delaying clock production for several frustrating weeks. This added blow complicated the problem already strained by the fire and the burden of the move to Ansonia. The firm became more deeply involved.

In order to help their deteriorating Ansonia operations, on July 26, 1856, Elias and Edward I of the town of Derby, and Andrew still of Bristol, mortgaged for $422 their charred factory property on North Main Street to the town of Bristol with a second mortgage held

The Purge of Fire

by the Ansonia Bank. In 1863 this property was sold to Nathan L. Birge, who later sold it back to Elias and Edward I for their clock factory home.

On September 9, 1856, in order to raise further capital, Edward I regretfully sold his Bristol house and lot on West Street to his father-in-law, Hammond Beach. This house was purchased and occupied in 1861 by young Mrs. Edward Ingraham I and family.

Conditions went from bad to worse at Ansonia. By November, the Ingrahams were forced to make an assignment. The brothers Andrew and Elias were about to disassociate, though, from unwanted circumstances. Never again would the initial "A" appear on an Ingraham clock. Andrew Ingraham would no more work in equality with his older brother. He would serve Elias only as an employee after 1869.

In 1856 Andrew maintained in Bristol sixteen acres, a house, one horse, two cattle, and one clock. Elias and Edward I were then propertyless in either the towns of Derby or Bristol. Andrew and Elias had spent 20 years together as partners through thick and thin, bankruptcies and prosperity. They temporarily parted as brothers deeper in kinship than mere blood ties could engender.

Yearning for a return to the tranquility of farm life, Andrew sold his Bristol home in January, 1860, moving to Guilford where the next month his wife, Rhoda, purchased a seventy-five acre farm on Clapboard Hill for $3,800. They remained in Guilford for nine years when they again returned to Bristol after selling their Guilford farm for $6,000 in April, 1869.

At the end of their financial rope, the Ingrahams filed a petition of bankruptcy in the New Haven probate court, December 1856. Sidney A. Downs and David Bassett were appointed trustees. The firm had farmed out some of its business after the fire. The trustees' report shows some goods at Plainville, work in process at Skinner and Barnes: 741 Round Gothic, 1,112 Sharp Gothic, and 2,900 Wellingtons; work at Holbrook and Tracy; 3,007 OG brass clocks; and finished work at Brainard and Funk.

The funereal accounting of the Ingraham Company dissolution on April 22, 1857, showed cash on hand of only $3,755.94 against staggering claims of $26,354.07, a net deficiency of $22,598.13.

Could the ill fortune which had twice forced Elias into bankruptcy be vanquished? Would his faith in himself and in his ability to design and sell clock cases again be resurrected?

Now fifty-two, would he be able yet to reap reward for his years of toil, reversal and struggle? How would his son, Edward, fare through his first baptism of failure?

In 1857 Edward Ingraham I, failing in health, disappointed, shaken by the bankruptcy, moved his family west, buying a farm in Jefferson, north of Chicago. Seeking a better climate and life, he raised vegetables for the city market. The records that would show the size, location and value of Edward's property in Cook County were destroyed in the great Chicago fire of 1871. After unsuccessfully farming he returned to Bristol about 1859, resuming with his father the manufacture of clocks which was his life work.

On April 25, 1857, William Shurtleff Ingraham, their second child, was born to Eliza and Edward Ingraham just before their trip west. Their eldest was Walter Andrew, born March 23, 1855, several months before the Ingraham factory fire.

Did Edward I's health fail from frustrations and rebellion augmented by anxiety from the fire and bankruptcy? As an only child, had he been reared in an atmosphere less conducive to the development of the toughness and resilience that was so apparent in his father and Uncle Andrew? Had his father's recent prosperity, albeit staggered twice by bankruptcy, softened this young man of twenty-seven? Edward I was all his life in relatively poor health. In spite of recurring frailty, he was destined to join his father in Ingraham Company management, contributing substantially to the firm's later success.

Though he was to be a life-long clockmaker, Edward I was descended from a line of farmers. He was the last Ingraham to show any interest in agriculture. When more affluent, he would spend much time and money on the Indian River farm in Florida experimenting with the growing of pineapple. He would also speculate on a sumptuous hotel at Martha's vineyard.

Putting aside clock company cares for a time, Elias heeded a call from his son and family out West. In 1858 he journeyed to the Chicago Ingraham farm for a visit with Edward I, his wife and their two young sons. Elias returned to Bristol with his eldest grandson, three-year-old Walter, who remained in his grandparents' home to be raised by Elias and Julia. Whether Edward I's infirmity or his failure as a farmer, or both, occasioned the transposition of Walter from his parental home to that of his grandfather's remains mute. If everything in the junior Ingraham home was harmonious, would not little Walter have remained there?

Further disturbing the already troubled Ingraham waters, Joseph Ingraham, Jr., Elias and Andrew's eighty-two-year-old father, died in Bristol, June 8, 1858. Elias' father was buried at Bristol's West Cemetery where his tombstone may yet be seen.

Edward I presently returned to Bristol where he joined his father in an infant clock company. From that time on much of the Ingraham Company business records appear in the son's own handwriting. He progressively assumed responsibility for company affairs and management, helping his father through the perplexities of war, boom and bust for the next quarter century. The partnership from 1860 to 1875 gave Elias two-thirds and Edward one-third.

Edward Ingraham I had grown up in the traditions of clockmaking and early showed an interest in his father's work. As a child he was greatly beloved by those associated with his father. After becoming actively interested in the business he was held in high regard. He entered the factory and made himself familiar with all the details of the manufacture of clocks. As time passed Elias turned over to Edward I, Walter and William more and more responsibility. They worked side by side to establish the Ingraham name.

Edward I, like his father, grew to become a quiet, unassuming man, not only just and fair but cordial and friendly towards those in his employ. He was a man of refined taste possessing a receptive mind and an excellent memory. He never seemed to be aware that his position in life was above that of any other upright, self-respecting citizen. He was a man and moved among men as one of them whatever their nationality or creed.

The public interest was ever close to Edward's heart. He welcomed and supported movements which promised to forward the public welfare and, although never seeking preferment of any kind, served his town and state when called on to do so.

The younger Ingraham represented Bristol in the state legislature in 1870. He was keenly interested in educational matters in the town and was a member of the board of state visitors. He also served on the board of Bristol Selectmen and Fire Commissioners. A family man, not

The Purge of Fire 159

robust, he annually paid $50 for military commutation and therefore escaped the rigors of the war between the states.

If the disastrous Ingraham factory fire in late 1855 had not ruined their clock business, the oncoming national depression of 1857 might have. Following the gold rush in California almost every line of business was overdone. This led to the depression. The clock business expanded during the early 1850s but clockmakers failed as the panic swept the nation. The paralysis took its toll among even such stalwarts as 50-year-old Jonathan Brown of Forestville near Bristol who made 100,000 clocks annually. In 1857 Bristol had more than sixty clock manufacturing concerns, many of which ceased business as a result of the panic beginning that year. Hardly would a recovery from the financial stringency occur before the young nation would be plunged into a bloody Civil War.

Could Elias again succeed after a second staggering business failure? Penniless, propertyless, but not pluckless, this spirited Yankee clockmaker was down but not out. His indomitable perseverance coupled with incredible mechanical and artistic skill and business judgment again organized a new clock company by 1857.

He first turned to his drawing board. Failing to patent the Sharp Gothic clock design, he determined not to let such an oversight happen again.

Between April, 1857, and June, 1871, at least eight original clock design patents were issued to Elias Ingraham by the United States Patent Office. Four were issued for cases known as Doric, Ionic, Venetian, and Grecian. These were the Ingraham breadwinners for many years, along with the Round and Sharp Gothics with their many variations. As before in the early 1840s when Elias was beaten, now again he used the vestibule between failure and reinstatement to develop new clock designs. With the thrown stones, he again built his own road to success.

In the spring of 1857, Elias began manufacturing his own patented clock cases in a Bristol case shop owned by Deacon Augustin Norton. Deacons Norton and William Day backed him financially. They agreed that the two Deacons should not be called on for any money but should wait until the clocks were sold before being repaid their $500 investment. Elias bought them out in 1861. Edward I then became his partner.

From a pile of refuse and charred pine and whitewood lumber salvaged from the 1855 fire, Elias made about 100 cases. With the profits he secured 1,000 feet of new lumber which was so frugally used that when cut up for cases, there was reportedly not enough remaining even to kindle a fire. The E. Ingraham and Company, phoenix-like, rose out of the alchemic ashes of failure stirred by an invincible Ingraham thrift and fired by his indomitable energy.

In October, 1857, Elias was no more financially affluent than he had been as an apprentice. He was without personal taxable property other than a time piece. E. Ingraham and Company already showed promise, being taxed on $500 for manufacturies. The next year the company doubled in value, tripled the third year. By 1859 Elias and one helper, possibly Edward I, finished 2,600 clock cases, the next year 5,000—primarily the column arch style. They used Pomeroy and Porter movements. Before leaving Ansonia Elias secured a patent on this style. Proving to be just what the market wanted, this clock made the business a success. Elias paid his help about $40 a month for a ten-hour day and a six-day week.

In 1860 Elisha Welch, Bristol's first millionaire, made 100,000 clocks annually. He exported large numbers to

The Purge of Fire 161

Europe, South America, China and Japan at an average of $2.50 each.

The 1860 census recorded Elias as being fifty-four, a manufacturer with business real estate valued at $1,600. Julia was listed merely as fifty-four. Their son Edward I was thirty, his wife, Janie, twenty-six, and their two sons Walter (five) and William (three). Edward I's third son, Irving, was born on December 6, 1860. This third child grew up to be irresponsible, and to some extent unstable while Walter and William were both a comfort and a help to their father and grandfather.

When Elias' third grandchild was born, Civil War clouds had gathered on the horizon. South Carolina seceded three months before President Elect Abraham Lincoln was inaugurated. The war ruined the lucrative clock market in the South. England and her colonies replaced the South as the leading clock market for Bristol clocks. After the war closed, prices rose, rents doubled, plants enlarged, real estate boomed and the Ingraham clock business was again off on a rising spiral. The Ingrahams were at the threshold of success for generations to come, though they knew it not at the time.

14

Thy Brother's Blood

1861-1872

The great inventor is one who has walked forth upon the industrial world, not from universities, but from hovels; not as clad in silks and decked with honors, but as clad in fustian and grimed with soot and oil.

—Isaac Taylor

As early as 1838 permission had been granted for antislavery society meetings to be held in the Bristol meeting house. Two years later the Abolition Party ran its first Presidential ticket, polling a mere thirty votes in the town. Pro-slavery sentiment stemmed from the close trade relations between Bristol and the South, by far its best clock market. Many Bristol clock traders who had been royally entertained on plantations absorbed the southern viewpoint, transmitting it to Bristol.

In 1864 Lincoln was reelected to the Presidency but not by Bristol voters who gave McClellan 395 to Lincoln's 327 votes. McClellan ran on a platform to end the war with recognition of the Confederate government. Whom did Elias, Andrew and Edward I vote for? Nobody knows.

Elias Ingraham and his son felt the initial suppression of the clock market followed by its rise into a new crescendo. In this period Elias designed such relatively small clocks (suitable for export) as the Venetian, Doric, and Ionic—noticeably smaller than those commonly made in the 1840s and 1850s and even later.

In 1921 Anna Ingraham, the widow of Irving Ingraham (Elias' grandson) shipped to William Ingraham (Irving's older brother) some furniture from their Los Angeles home. Much of this furniture—chairs, tables, mirrors and clocks—was the handiwork of Elias. In this shipment was Elias' favorite clock, which he had designed and made in about 1828 for George Mitchell. This clock is now displayed in the American Clock Museum in Bristol.

Edward Ingraham II owns a drop leaf table from among these effects. The table had a drawer with a broken pull. In 1965 he wrote:

> One day I put the drawer in the car and went to Goodsell's Junk Yard on North Street to see if I could find a replacement. Found none. On the way home I stopped to call on Reggie Morrell (then a curator of the American Clock and Watch Museum) who sat in the car for a visit. As he got into the car, I put the drawer into the back seat but turned it over . . . and to our astonishment on the bottom of the drawer there had been sketched with a pair of calipers a design for the sash such as was used on the Ventian clock and for which Elias had received a design patent in 1861. Certainly sure proof to me that this table was made by Elias.

Fifteen days after Abraham Lincoln was inaugurated, the United States Patent Office issued to Elias Ingraham a patent for a new clock style, the Venetian. Its sash was sketched on the drawer bottom of the drop leaf table.

Shortly after E. and A. Ingraham's bankruptcy of 1856 Elias patented two new clocks. In addition to the Venetian, patents were issued on three other styles in 1861, one each in 1862, three in 1870, one in 1871 and one in 1873 just prior to his trip to California.

Edward Ingraham I was thirty-one, with a wife and children, when the Civil War broke out. He paid for and held a military commutation during the Civil War. His library of art and travel indicated a sophistication of interest repulsed by the carnage of battlefields. In 1862 he owned a house, even a piano.

Elias at fifty-six, too old for military service, worked on new clock designs, made clocks and put down roots for the munificent years ahead. At this period he retained his luxuriant head of red hair now tinged with gray. His forehead was broad and high, nose large and strong, mouth wide and determined, chin firm, blue-green eyes gentle with a slight twinkle. His hands were artistic, his fingers supple, long and sensitive. His posture was erect, his manner vigorous and disciplined, his bearing noble.

Written from Shrewsbury, Massachusetts, to Elias and Julia by Honora Sparks Andrews (Julia Ingraham's sister) is a letter dated May 17, 1863, revealing much of the cruelty of the Civil War. Honora begins: "My Dear Brother & Sister," and speaks of her solicitous affection for Julia and Elias. Honora, a newly arrived resident of Shrewsbury, continues:

> I am enjoying myself very well, quite as well as I could expect among straingers, it is not so pleasant to be all the time forming new acquaintances, but we can conform to almost anything if we make up the mind to do so. My health is better than it was before i was sick, though I am not worth mutch, I think I shall lose all my hair, it falls off by handfulls.

Thy Brother's Blood

Such reference was to one of the communicable plagues that spent itself in 19th century New England. Honora speaks of a trip to Boston taken by herself and doctor husband. She writes, "There were two companies out, one cald the Lancets, they were all mounted on beautiful horses. A great many spectators, it was a sight for me."

Begging the Ingrahams to visit her, she writes,

> If you should go to Boston and feel if you could possibly afford the time to stop with us a while your best way would be to stop in Worcester as there is no regular line or stage from the other places. There is a regular stage from Worcester to Shrewsbury . . . . It gits here about five . . . . Unless they have a full load they come in an hour. The fair is 25 cts. We should be extremely glad to see both of you. Elias I think when you take your fall ture you can take Julia along with you as far as here and make us a visit then go on to the vineyard and so on leaving Julia to meet you in Hartford on your return.

The reference to Elias' "fall ture" shows not only Honora's phonetic spelling but confirms Elias had regularly visited Martha's Vineyard before 1863.

The plight of villages in the depths of the War Between the States is pathetically seen from these comments by Honora:

> We had a Lavee here last thursday evening to raise money for the Soldiers or in other words, to raise money to buy cloth's so that we can make cloth's for their comefort. We raised clean, along hundred seventy five dollars. There is scarcely a young man in town. Our milkman says he has seven brothers in the army. There were nine of them, himself and one more is all there is left at home. Two and three out of a family here is nothing strange. When will this terrible war end?

Honora speaks of Edward I's eldest eight-year-old son, Walter, who lived with his grandparents, Elias and Julia:

> Tell Walter I have put a beautiful picture of a little girl opposite his in my album. They look well together. We think your are very fine. I don't think Julia had better say she cant have a good picture.

That Julia was not photogenic may be seen by her pictures which show her to be of rather stern countenance as were those of her sisters.

Honora then speaks of her doctor husband's practice, "doing good business since we came here. The first month he booked more than fifty dolars and took the greater part of it in cash. He has several cases of scarlet fever. They have all done well and all think there never was such a good doctor."

Forty-five years before, Dr. Andrew married Honora Sparks then a girl of 17. Little did Honora know that she herself, as a widow a dozen years hence, would share the name Ingraham for in 1875 she became Andrew Ingraham's third and last wife.

During the 15 years following the Civil War, headlong assaults were made on three aspects of public taste: on interior decoration, architecture and art appreciation. The Gothic style carried through the mid part of the century. The Queen Anne or Elizabethan then battled the Gothic and won. The 1876 Philadelphia Centennial effected the marriage of industry and household arts. Elias exhibited many of his original clock styles at that centennial.

The building boom which followed the Civil War further accelerated the change from the Gothic, turning thought from the classical to inexpensive jigsaw fussiness and into less romantic taste. The vacation home Elias

Thy Brother's Blood

built at Cottage City in Martha's Vineyard shows how strongly he still embraced the Gothic.

By 1865 Elias rode high the road to prosperity as witnessed by the Bristol *Press* on July 31, 1890.

> The clock business as well as the industries of the county were very prosperous during the war and the succeeding years when everybody made money, this company [Ingraham] being no exception and the intensive trade thus favorably opened has ever since continued in a large degree, the company having steadily increased its business until the present time.

In the bankruptcy of 1856 the Ingraham's Bristol factory property and water rights were mortgaged to the city and later sold to Nathaniel Birge. In 1865 Birge sold it back to Elias to use for the Ingraham Clock Shop expansion.

After the war clock materials dropped in price. The savings were passed along by the Ingrahams to their customers, as the list on page 168 reveals.

All of these familiar styles sprang from the fertile talent of Elias Ingraham. Likely the pricing derived from his astute thirty-five-year-old son, Edward I.

After nearly a decade without personal real estate, on February 19, 1866, Elias bought a house at the corner of North Street and Burlington Avenue including the "Ingraham Hill" land which he later laid out in building lots. The fortunes of the Ingrahams indeed improved, and now Julia and grandson Walter moved into Elias' newly acquired house. For forty years, Elias had worked, waited, watched, won, lost, won again. Forty years of struggles, forty years of reverses, forty years with a few bright spots had flown by. Now he was to be rewarded for those years of tireless toil, self-discipline and patient persistence.

Revised Price List
of
E. INGRAHAM & CO.,
Bristol, Conn., June 1st, 1865.

In consequence of the reduced cost of materials used in the manufacture of Clocks, we have decided to make a corresponding reduction in our quotations, and have established the following as the lowest sales for our goods at the factory, from this date.

Eight Day Venetian	$5.25
" " " Extra	5.50
" " " " Gilt	5.75
" " " No. 2	4.75
" " " " " Extra	5.00
" " " " " " Gilt	5.25
" " " Column Arch	5.50
" " " " Gilt	5.75
" " Grecian	6.25
" " Ionic Time	5.00
" " " " Gilt	6.50
" " " Strike	5.75
" " " " Gilt	7.25
One Day Venetian	3.75
" " " Extra Gilt	4.25
" " Small Venetian	3.25
" " " " Gilt	3.75
" " Doric	3.00
" " Grecian	4.00
" " Venetian Time	2.10

Alarms, 50 cents additional.

By 1870, exclusive of clock company investments, Elias owned personal property assessed at $5,450, including two houses, four acres, three dogs, musical instruments and $250 in "quarries, fisheries, and mines." The Ingraham Company was valued at $23,450, including houses, stores, mills, factories and inventories.

Had Elias retired at sixty, he would have been denied major fruition. Retirement would have condemned him to unknelled anonymity and otherwise deprived generations to come of livelihood from the Ingraham backbone. A great institution profiles a great man, and the Ingraham Company indeed beshadowed Elias and his indomitable spirit.

Elias felt concern for his family as his fortune soared, for on January 24, 1866, he purchased a policy from Charter Oak Life Insurance Company of Hartford. For a $169.50 premium he owned life insurance for the next twelve months in an unknown amount, though it must have been substantial for those days. Life insurance was not then fashionable. Elias did not renew it. He was too much a tight-fisted Yankee to sustain much dependence and besides, he was really on the way in the clock business.

Although the Pecks were active Bristol insurance agents, Elias, with customary independence, later procured life insurance from a Danbury, Connecticut, agent. In his original spelling, Elias, dissatisfied, wrote:

Bristol Jany 19th 1878

John Tweedy Esqr

Der Sir   Your Kinde letter of the 18th instant is received In Which You Wish to know what I intend to do. I have told you My Experience in this line of insureance up to this time until I have lost all hart in it. I have concluded to stop paying in any More Enstallments. You say that All that I have invested in this N.Y. Life insurance is Safely invested. I shall expect all My interest protected in it

Yours Truley
Elias Ingraham

E. Ingraham and Company made cases for a few years and bought movements from other manufacturers. Then they found that a better clock was demanded in the market. To furnish clocks of the desired quality, Elias made his own movements. Accordingly he bought an old hardware shop. The first machinery, including lathes and some tools for making clock parts, was taken from Charles Foote's old shop in Bristol.

Anson Atwood, a skilled movement maker, was induced to leave his farm in 1865 and again take charge of the movement shop. He was Ingraham's superintendent for more than twenty years, and under his supervision the Ingraham clock movements held a high reputation in the market, both at home and abroad. Atwood had worked for Brewster and Ingrahams as a movement maker back in the late 1840s and early 1850s.

On October 30, 1867, Maude Ingraham, fifth grandchild of Elias, was born to Eliza and Edward Ingraham. Maude Ingraham Herendeen died in 1950. A widow, she was bright, gay, idiosyncratic.

As General Grant became President in March, 1869, the country floundered in a post-war turmoil prior to the panic of 1873. About three months after Grant's inauguration Leland Stanford with a Nevada silver sledge tapped a California gold spike into a polished laurel railroad tie. That blow at Utah's Promontory Point activated a telegraph key which clattered across the nation: "Done." The first transcontinental railroad was finished. The nation was now spanned with iron rails. The great publicity generated therefrom beckoned Elias to California in 1873. Ingraham clocks were now readily marketed in the mighty West.

On November 17, 1869, the Suez Canal officially

opened. Suddenly the Orient was now weeks closer to Connecticut clock companies.

As the Ingraham Company flourished through the seventies, the day-by-day management evolved more and more upon capable Edward I. By the 1880s Elias' grandsons, Walter and William, assisted in management. After 1870 Edward I did the accounting and correspondence. Unjaded at seventy, Elias went to the shop to work with his bench tools as well as on the drawing board. As the principal owner, taking less and less a hand in daily affairs, he nevertheless participated in important company decisions. It was before the day of retirement at sixty-five.

After a ten-year absence from Bristol, Andrew Ingraham sold the Guilford farm and returned to Bristol in 1870. He dealt in water wheels, patented by Joel Case. Elias and Edward I substantially invested in Andrew's Bristol dealership. Andrew was not too successful since steam was replacing falling water as the source of industrial power. To supplement his income, Andrew was sexton at the Bristol Congregational Meeting House, where he earned $2.25 per day. By 1870 he owned a house and four acres, a horse and carriage and $2,800 in "money at interest in this state and elsewhere."

When did the Ingraham factory change from water power to steam? On the north bank of the Pequabuck River the E. & A. Ingraham plant at the time of the 1855 fire was powered by water wheels fed through Birge's Pond, once known as Ray's Pond, named after Benjamin Ray who formed the clockmaking firm of Ray and Ingraham in 1841. An Ingraham Company letter dated December 15, 1871, complained to the Roper Company of the trouble with their caloric engine. The next year various letters to H. B. Bigelow Company of New Haven were written regarding steam boilers, used to supply caloric engines with steam. Steam replaced water power in the Ingraham factory in the late 1860s or early 1870s. Electricity, either for power or light, was not used in the factory during Elias' lifetime.

William Ingraham, second son of Edward I, recalled that his grandmother, Julia Ingraham, used to say, "Go it while you are young because when you are old you can't." Some of Edward I's business speculations indicate that he heeded it as well. He was not always a wise or careful investor.

In the 1870s Martha's Vineyard off Cape Cod was not only a retreat for temperate Elias but a place of speculation for his immoderate son. In 1872, Edward I invested the prodigious sum of $10,000 for a half interest in a 650-lot tract on the west side of the lagoon. Former school teacher, hard-boiled clockmaker and industrialist, William Gilbert (1806–1890) of Winsted joined him. He bought for five thousand dollars a one-third interest which he later sold for one dollar to Wallace Barnes. Patent holder of the water wheels sold by Andrew Ingraham, Joel Case, in 1876 built on their Vineyard property a Victorian hotel called the Oklahoma Hall. Suffering from lack of financial resources and other reversals, the venture was unsuccessful. Edward I lost his investment in this Vineyard speculation. The hotel was later destroyed by fire in 1897.

Another of Edward I's unsuccessful ventures was that of the American Coal Barge Company, which mechanically loaded and unloaded coal barges. His unwise investments in the 1870s remind one of Elias' calamitous speculation with the Hayes invalid chair of the late 1830s.

The Reverend Charles H. Riggs, an occasional preacher at the Bristol Congregational Church, borrowed forty dollars each from Elias Ingraham, N. L. Birge, Joseph Peck and J. H. Sessions and on March 9, 1871, began to publish the weekly Bristol *Press*. Out of the first year's profits, Riggs paid off the investors.

Printed on an old Washington hand press, the first issue recorded among other things that there were 61,000 clergymen of all denominations in the country who were paid an average of $700 annual salary. It contained also an account of Elisha Brewster's eightieth birthday celebration. Anyone now for starting a newspaper with $160?

July 27, 1871, found Elias at Vineyard Grove, Martha's Vineyard. That Elias hungered for news about Bristol is seen from a postscript to a letter to Edward I: "Doo orders increase How are you getting along . . . ."

Elias' poignant comments about the happy life on the Vineyard and his reluctance to return to Bristol's "Musketoes and Flies" is understandable. He was comforted to know that he could leave company affairs for a while in the capable hands of Edward I and be released for a time from "the care and perplexety of business."

Referring to the remodeling of the Bristol meeting house he wrote, "They are just about finishing the Chappel I would like to see it completed and our Butiful clock put up in it."

Referring to a Vineyard church, he continued,

> I put up the Chesnut 18 inch over the Prechers stand yesterday it appears well their . . . the Bluff side has improved verry much since last season. The Chappel makes a center and brings us in it it increases the value of property around it.

Elias' reference to an improvement in real estate values on the Bluff side leads to the conjecture that not only Edward but Elias himself may have been involved in land speculation on the Vineyard. Like son, like father!

The Bristol Congregational Meeting House, then nearly forty years old, underwent its first remodeling. The outstanding change was the new pews. Calvinism began to show a modest retirement as seen from this comment written by the editor of the Bristol *Press* on August 18, 1871:

> If you have never read that pew doors are an abomination unto the Lord it does not alter the fact that they are so. Last Sunday was our last pew door service. No more will these doors tear dresses, pinch fingers, squeak on their hinges, or form a barricade on which the captain of the pew reposes for a nap. No more will little shavers hide behind them to eat nuts and whisper. No more will we see a pew holder hold the door to shut out a stranger or poor neighbor.

The call of the wild West came to Elias in early 1873. In his sixty-eighth year, temporarily poor in health, with the clock company in the able hands of his son, Elias turned westward to see at first hand the mighty West, wild Indians, buffalo, and the then rough and ready California pioneers.

15

Riding the Rails Westward

1873

The world is a great book, of which they who never stir from home read only a page.
—Augustine

As Elias contemplated his 1873 California trip, twenty-year-old Walter Ingraham, his eldest grandson, started to work at five cents an hour in the old wooden case shop of the Ingraham Company. The next year he was promoted to the office. By 1880 he would become secretary of the company. Upon the death in 1892 of his father, Edward I, Walter became the president for thirty-five years. Like his grandfather, he was modest, unassuming and retiring, keen and observing. Reared by Elias and Julia, Walter made a definite contribution to the success of the company which was to last for generations still to come.

The Bristol *Press* of June 19, 1873, printed an account of Elias' return home from California:

Home again—Mr. Elias Ingraham returned from California last Wednesday evening very much improved in health. During the past month he has visited the Yo-Semite Valley and other places of interest.

On Thursday, July 3, the *Press* published a letter from Elias written a few days before:

Mr. Editor—

Home again, as you say in your issue of June 19th—yes, home again—and I do appreciate it very much, I do assure you, it is so pleasant to meet old friends again, and enjoy their society. I wish especially to express my gratitude to the Bristol Cornet Band for the serenade and hearty welcome they gave me on the evening of the 13th.

And again, on the evening of the 27th, they appeared on the stand in my grove and discoursed sweet music to us and our neighborhood, all of which is highly appreciated. It is with me something as it was with a lady whom I once met who had previously lived in Bristol but had bought a farm and moved into another town; they could not have anything quite so good as they used too—their potatoes were not so mealy and luscious, their vegetables in general were not so sweet and good as those they raised in Bristol. I have heard a number of bands play in Anaheim, Sacramento and San Francisco, but the music of none of them was as sweet and agreeable to me as that of our Bristol Band. Success to you, dear Band, as with the goldheaded cane.

Elias Ingraham

Walter Ingraham inherited this goldheaded cane given to Elias by those working with him in 1873.

Referring to his great-grandfather's California trip, Edward Ingraham II says,

Elias probably took the one transcontinental railroad then available. I have a hunch he was of an adventuresome spirit and wanted to see where the deer and the

Riding the Rails Westward

antelope roam, to see real, raw Indians, the Yosemite, the Tetons, and California, where some of his compatriots ventured in the rush of '49. I doubt if he went via the Isthmus or Straits of Magellan or that Walter went with him. Walter does not seem to me to have been either athletic or adventuresome. I don't have any idea Julia was with him. She often was not. I think he went to California because he wanted to see it (health secondary), enjoy the new country and experiences. At about 68 he must have been strong and rugged. His early pictures give one the impression of physical strength and courage. He must have had guts. There were a lot of '49ers out of Connecticut and he must have heard tales from more than one of them.

At least one " '49er" from Bristol was George Bartholomew (1805-1897). He returned home in 1853 and likely spun yarns to Elias and others for the next twenty years, about California grandeur, whetting their traveling appetites.

In this Indian Summer period of Elias' life, time was not of the essence since his son and others managed the company in its day-to-day affairs. Likely Elias went to California on four-year-old Union Pacific-Central Pacific Railroad cars. Elias rode in hard-seated cars heated by iron stoves that roasted those near and froze those beyond. He dined en route at railside dining rooms. George Pullman had recently designed elegant and comfortable railroad cars. His ideas came from ship rather than carriage design. Trained like Elias as a cabinet maker, Pullman revolutionized railroad car making. The first Pullman car was introduced to the Transcontinental Line the very year that Elias made his trip west. Whale oil or kerosene headlights were used on the woodburning, steam-engined "ironhorses."

En route by rail to California Elias Ingraham passed

through Chicago, a roughneck of a city, and witnessed its uneven development of opulence and poverty, saw its planked sidewalks and unpaved streets, smelled stockyard's stench, and felt the vigorous, exciting atmosphere of this vortex of rawness and culture. He beheld charred evidences of the fire which had nearly destroyed the city only a year and a half before.

On Friday, April 13, while Elias was absent, the Bristol *Press* reported the burning of the Seymour & Nott block—perhaps the most disastrous fire that ever occurred in Bristol. The Tuesday before, another fire blazed in nearby Forestville, destroying the clock case and finishing shops of Welch Spring Company, an Ingraham competitor. Such fires were reminiscent of the disastrous 1855 fire which threw the Ingrahams into bankruptcy. Someone evidently wrote Elias about the fires, for the *Press* of May 9, 1873, reported,

> We have received a letter from California from Mr. Elias Ingraham dated at Sacramento Cal. April 26th in which he says: "Give my kind regards to all my friends in Bristol, especially to those who have recently been burned out. They have my warmest sympathy."

"Warmest sympathy?" Was Elias injecting a little dry, Yankee humor into his letter? Edward I would have and so would have his grandson Edward II.

As Elias threaded his way westward on the Union Pacific, beyond Omaha, he saw on the plains dainty, graceful antelope, prairie dog villages, coyotes, jack rabbits, prairie hens, ghost towns reminiscent of railhead days. He beheld the sweeping grandeur of the rising prairie, still dotted with a million buffalo.

Elias Ingraham was in Sacramento on April 23, 1873, "a windy, cold, rainy day." Founded the year before Elias' first bankruptcy, Sacramento boomed after gold was discovered nearby in 1848. The Big Four—Crocker, Stanford, Hopkins and Huntington—brought the railroad over the Sierra range just four years before. It is likely that Elias Ingraham knew of Collis Potter Huntington (1821-1900) who was born in Harwinton, Connecticut, ten miles northwest of Bristol. The fifth of nine children, Huntington at fifteen had been a Yankee peddler, selling watches and watch findings in the South. He later found himself railroading in California. Did Elias look him up in Sacramento?

As Elias entered Sacramento, a city of 20,000 so different from his native Bristol, he beheld tree-lined streets, the newly completed half-granite, half-brick capital building, groves of orange, olive and fig trees, blooming flowers, brick, wood, white and yellow adobe houses, wooden arcades, plank sidewalks, a dirty Chinese quarter, wide-verandahed hotels, the great Sacramento River with whistling steamers and laboring barges.

It is likely on such a steamer as *S. M. Whipple* that Elias sailed down the Sacramento River into the chill San Francisco Bay, docking at one of the piers along the Embarcadero at the city by the Golden Gate. Did he eat one or more of those fifty-cent dinners, sleep in a fifty-cent berth, and listen to the calliopist on board?

En route he would have sailed past the 150-foot-high guano-covered rock, Alcatraz (Spanish for "pelican"). Later the rock was famous as a maximum security federal prison, a twelve-acre island, formerly a Spanish fortress and dungeon. It served in 1873 as a military prison.

Visitors like Elias paid fifty cents a night for a single hotel room and four or five dollars a week for board, either walked or rode horse-drawn street cars or private carriages to see roaring San Francisco in its rugged beautiful setting of sand dune and sin, its buildings clinging to sides of abrupt hills along some of the steepest streets in the world. There Chinese junks, brigs, barks, full-rigged ships, even river boats brought in the '49ers only twenty-four years before. Many gold seekers, like Bartholomew from Bristol, walked overland, came in battered covered wagons, or sailed to San Francisco.

Ship passage just from New Orleans to San Francisco had been $300 in 1849. During the gold craze the blacksmith dropped his hammer, carpenter his plane, mason his trowel, farmer his sickle, baker his loaf, tapster his bottle, even Bristol clockmakers their tools. All went off to the mines, some on horses, some in carts, some on crutches. Soldiers deserted. Fifty thousand miners drifted on the Sierra slopes, sought gold in the summer, a motley, restless, rummaging, roving, ragged multitude of adventurers. Many remained even after the gold petered out by 1854.

The 1872 Bancroft Guide advertised The Pacific Mail Steamship Company: "Steamer leaves San Francisco for Hong Kong from the companies wharf foot of Brannan and First Streets, on the first of each month at twelve o'clock noon . . . ." The fare was $100 steerage, $300 first class. Elias with his adventuresome spirit may well have been tempted by the Hong Kong sailing, though he confined his adventure to perhaps just a California coastal trip, as we shall see.

San Francisco still showed evidence of an earthquake the year before when hundreds of shocks occurred, ripping chasms four feet in width, cascading rocks down the mountains with sparks flying, while streams reversed their flow.

The first Clay Street cable car began operation in the fog on August 1, soon after Elias returned to Connecticut. He missed a five-cent ride on the gallant little cable cars that a century later were still in use and ridden by his touring descendants. However, on June 2, Elias could have witnessed the groundbreaking for the first street cable railway in the world there in San Francisco. The mechanical cars were the result of the hilly terrain making horse-drawn vehicles impractical or impossible. Andrew Hallidie's cable cars rapidly replaced those horse-drawn as public means of transportation. In 1869 Hallidie, walking up a San Francisco hill on a cold winter day, saw on the cobblestones a car drawn by four ironshod horses. One horse slipped and fell, the car running backwards dragged and injured the horses cruelly.

Hurt by this scene, Hallidie, with a humanitarian instinct, drawing from his cable experience, invented a car that would move up and down hill by cables driven by steam power.

At this time the North Pacific Transportation Company charged nine dollars steerage and eighteen dollars first class from San Francisco to San Diego, a seventy-hour voyage undertaken every sixth day. The daily stage run south to Pueblo de Los Angeles being rugged, it is likely that Elias used the sea rather than land when traveling to Anaheim, and likely he went first class, not steerage. He would have disembarked at Anaheim Landing, and been taken ashore on a lighter from the ship standing off in the open ocean.

Started in 1857, Anaheim had been a colonial venture founded by San Francisco Germans, fourteen carpenters, four blacksmiths, three watchmakers, a brewer, engraver, shoemaker, poet, miller, bookbinder, two or three merchants, a hatter, musician and hostler. Claiming to be the first city in the United States to have advanced planning prior to occupation, the colony was laid out in small farms on a portion of a Spanish grant twenty-eight miles southeast of Los Angeles, then a pueblo of but a few thousand souls. Thirteen miles west of the colony the port, Anaheim Landing, had been established in 1864.

Yosemite 1873: spring . . . grassy meadows . . . sage-covered mesas . . . melting snow . . . cascading waterfalls . . . gossamer haze . . . Bridal Veil . . . Vernal . . . Nevada . . . Yosemite and Ribbon Falls . . . plunging . . . Cathedral Rock . . . Mirror Lake . . . Half Dome . . . ice-carved canyons . . . giant Sequoias . . . heaving, swelling sea of green . . . wild flowers . . . bear . . . deer . . . perilous trails—Yosemite 1873!

On October 18, 1965, Norman Bishop, museum curator of Yosemite National Park, wrote:

> We finally had an opportunity to pull the Grand Register out of the Museum display case. It weighs 100 pounds, and found no signature for Elias Ingraham from those among Connecticut. The earliest entry from that state was July 21, 1873 . . .

Did Elias sleep out among the trees?

In spite of the absence of a documented account by Mr. Bishop that Elias reached Yosemite in 1873 we have Elias Ingraham's own report that he was there in late spring of that year. Though sixty-eight, he rode in a saddle since no stage yet had rolled into the valley.

First seen by white man in 1849, named for an Indian tribe, the greatest national curiosity in the state, Yosemite had been much publicized in Eastern newspapers after 1865. Such publicity as this from the Bancroft Guide of 1872 must have reached Elias in far-away New England, whetting his desire to behold the valley.

In June, 1855, six months before the disastrous Ingraham clock company fire in Bristol, the first white tourists to Yosemite were James Hutchings and an artist. At Mariposa they engaged two Indian guides who took

Riding the Rails Westward

them on an obscure trail to the awesome Yosemite Valley, where they spent five days taking notes and making drawings. Hutchings then wrote of the Yosemite in *California Magazine,* exciting curiosity and giving to the world its first verbal and graphic pictures of the famed 4,000-foot-high valley.

In the *Appleton Magazine* of 1873, James Hutchings promoted the 200-mile, two-day "speedy" Coulterville route to Yosemite. "Comfortable and safe," carried by rail and stage from San Francisco to Yosemite, "without horseback riding" visitors were transported on private teams and stage the last eighty-eight miles.

Without horseback riding? Not likely. At Yosemite, Hutchings had a saw mill and visitor accommodations in a rickety hotel and sheep herder shacks.

By 1865, 369 visitors had seen the marvelous valley and its waterfalls. By 1869, more than 1,000 saw them. John Muir, Scotch naturalist and author, worked in Yosemite for Hutchings as a sawyer until two years before Elias' trip.

Although few Californians went to Yosemite, out-of-staters were expected to go and Elias with an adventuresome spirit, did.

Elias experienced the rigors of the Yosemite trip but it is unlikely that his sturdy Yankee self-discipline and natural vigor would have answered Olive Logan's journalistic question, "Does it Pay to Visit Yo Semite?" other than, "Yes! Yes! Yes!"

You there, Elias Ingraham, astride that plodding, sweating surefooted mule carrying you upward, onward to the mighty mountain. After the ink of night see the cool grey dawn breaking yonder, the sunrise like cosmetics of Spirit painting the cheeks of clouds. Watch the picturesque, noiseless, inexorable climb of noonday thunderheads in azure frame. Do those clouds recall to you the graceful arc of your steeple clocks, the wide face of the sky and endless mountain?

Note now the undivined imprisonment of the top-knotted quail. Thither hear his cheery call. Does it all hint of the imprisonment equally unknown to itself of a metronomic escapement cheerfully tick-tocking within hollowed chambers? Or are you enthralled only with the trail, the squeak of leather, the ocean of vendure, the thrill of life in these majestic Sierra surrounds? Likely it is your present precincts, rather than past performance, that pervades your spirit, captures your imagination, nourishes your soul.

Observe there, Yankee clockmaker, columns of fir and pine and spruce, ten—nay, twenty times—higher than your first cabinet shop, rising skyward from trunks thick as a wagon length, 100 feet to the first limb. In miniature do they suggest a vision of your own slender pillared Gothic clocks?

Hear those whispered requiems from pine-needled, scented forests undulating to and fro. Do they recall to you the rhythm of your own clocks? Do the bells and chimes of yon warblers in field and meadow remind you of the stayed ringing on the half and on the hour of your timings?

Ponder how the great Architect of nature designing this mightiness of glacial enormity and towering fir trees patiently serving as shadow and food and shelter and comfort to His little ones, just as your life work will serve, nay *has* served, as shadow and food and shelter and comfort to your little ones for generations to come.

See there those deep woods monarched with thousand-year-old giants surrounded by glens of their wooded children. We, but not you, know of children, not wooden but human, who will be surrounded and blessed by windfalls your talent and bravery began.

Riding the Rails Westward

Hear now, Elias, the singing bees within that cavernous tree like a hollowed clock chamber alive with a cadence of metallic insects of coil and stroke. Are you not in tune with the artistry of God's handiwork in nature here before you? You have reflected in your own life work nature's symmetry and grace frozen into mahogany and walnut and pine and oak and birch and cherry in fifty score styles of clock cases. Do those great Sequoias silently, tirelessly mantling mountain typify to you your clocks bedecking mantles above a thousand thousand hearths?

See there now the mountainside like a verdant wall of God's living room, that stone shelf shining like black slate, the furniture unfashioned by human hand, already designed and built and carved, serving as sentinels of comfort. Behold the graceful, swirling limbs of yon juniper. Are they not faintly likened to the hands on the dials of your own clocks rotating around the face of the dial? Note well how spring winds up nature to release blossom and song and mating and nesting as clocks are wound to release the telling of time, the sound of chime and bell, the constant tick-tocking of their escapement.

See there that mirrored lake, "the smile of God," as Indians say, its shores with upturned corners of expressive joy, another like the eye of Soul skyward peering through eyelashes of pinioned pine. Below lies a valley like God's footstool, above lies the mountain like His chair, fragrant, pine-cushioned for comfort. See now the change in sky furniture as noontide clouds weep with soulful joy from loving eyes that knoweth even the sparrow's flight.

Now, Elias Ingraham, for joy have you mounted this rugged trail to Yosemite. Without melancholy remember trails of twenty, forty, even fifty years back, when patience, persistence and purposefulness involving survival, not pleasure, were your trial. Like the life of these mountains yours has sometimes been torment when drought hushed the fount, when fire blackened an already dark night with fearful flame. But like the forest you quietly returned after fire to move forward, where perchance one day fires may burn but to warm and comfort, never again to destroy or brand. Nature's tools—glacier, wind, water, frost, and fire have molded this Yosemite monument while your instruments—water wheel, bellows, lathes, saws, glue have molded the Gothic, the Venetian, the Ionic, the Doric, the Corinthian, the Grecian as Ingraham monuments also for generations to come.

As the waters of Yosemite flow to make productive valleys yet to be watered beyond, so you, Elias, have labored not only for yourself but beyond for the benefit of generations unborn, and now you must, you do, suspect your work may continue even beyond a grave. We know it, and love and honor and respect you a hundred years hence.

"Our life, exempt from public haunt, finds tongues in trees, books in the running brooks, sermons in stones and good in everything."

16

Harvest Years

1874-1880

In sickness let me not so much say, am I getting better of my pain? as am I getting better for it?

—Shakespeare

On September 22, 1874, Rhoda Barber Ingraham, age sixty-eight, died at Bristol and widowed Andrew, her husband for thirty-six years. Rhoda's will dated April 20, 1872, witnessed among others by Elias Ingraham, began: "In the name of God! Amen!" She bequeathed the bulk of her estate of some substance to her faithful husband.

Having now lost his second wife, Andrew remained a widower for a little less than a year. On July 18, 1875, he married Honora Sparks Andrews, Julia's elder widowed sister. He was her second husband, she his third and last wife.

Honora Sparks Ingraham lived until September 14, 1879. Augustus Funk found this regarding her funeral: "September 16, age 77, size 5 feet 6 inches tall, casket $50, hearse $3." Funeral costs had risen $11 in 5 years. Andrew lived the 15-year remainder of his life a widower.

The older members of the Ingraham family now remember Andrew with a nose cancer in his latter days. It is said that for this unhappy reason individual communion cups came into use at the Bristol Congregational Church. My mother-in-law, Faith Ingraham Treadway, remembers her great-great uncle Andrew sitting in the "Amen pew" with a bandage over his disfigured nose.

Later he is remembered as noseless from an apparent surgical operation. Asked then if he could breathe all right, taciturn Andrew replied, "I can, Sir."

E. Ingraham and Company now occupied wooden buildings on the east side of Bristol's North Main Street. With his son Edward I as partner, Elias continued to work marvels in clock production and sales. They put the best designs on the market with clock works of superior quality, shipping not only domestically but to Europe, Asia, and South America.

In 1880 the E. Ingraham and Company incorporated as a joint stock company. Elias was president.

During the '70s and '80s the company bought carloads of eastern white pine of a so-called box grade from dealers in Tonawanda, New York and Boston. Oak, whitewood, walnut and Mahogany stacked three to six months to dry, were first hauled by rail then by team to the company lumber yard except during the spring muddy season. At any one time, a million and a half feet of lumber were stored at the Ingraham mill, abundant evidence of the magnitude of their clock business. Boards were planed, then cut into lengths required for fabrication and shipping of clocks. Sawdust from kerf was spread on the shop floors to absorb oil from the automatic screw machines in the turning rooms. Wood shavings used for packing clocks were secured in fifteen-pound parcels. Corrugated cardboard cartons for packing were not used in the Ingraham Company until the 1920s.

Harvest Years

In the 1920s there was a prodigious amount of clock gilding done by as many as thirty gilders applying gold leaf in a skillful manner. Although this art in Bristol dated as early as 1840, it reached its apex in the late '70s and early '80s when Ingrahams exported many clocks to China where Orientals demanded gilded clocks. The 1849 gold rush was modestly replaced by a Bristol gilt rush thirty years later, and the Ingrahams were in the thick of it.

Bearded and mustachioed blue-eyed Edward Ingraham I was a practical joker. He loved to travel. As an adult he was in chronic poor health. We have already seen after the 1857 bankruptcy in Ansonia how he moved to Chicago for his health.

Edward II recalls:

Edward Ingraham I and Wallace Barnes were close friends. Wallace chewed tobacco. When Edward built a new house it is said that he had the first plate glass window in town. The house, two-story and pretentious, was in the 100 block on Summer Street. He is said to have invited Wallace over and sat him down before the plate glass window. Wallace had a chew. When he got his gullet full, he spit all over the plate glass window thinking he was out of doors. Another time in the spring Wallace insisted Edward come over and get some of his fine cabbages. So Edward appeared, presumably with wheel barrow and Wallace led him down to the brook where "skunk cabbages" were growing in profusion, probably to Edward's confusion . . . .

Another story is to the effect that Elias objected to the men spending any time cleaning up around the shop. This was non-productive labor. The old case shop, however, got pretty dirty. There was a large stove in the center of the shop which, of course, was a dangerous condition.

The men, realizing the situation, not liking the disorder, contrived to move all the shavings, debris and scrap towards Elias' bench until finally he gave up in despair and all hands cleaned house.

Edward I bought some land in the Florida Indian River country where he started a pineapple plantation. Pineapple planting had been introduced from Havana to Florida about 1860.

Edward's pineapple plantation, like others in Florida, did poorly. After his father's death, Edward I docked at his Indian River plantation a fifty-foot, $5,000 houseboat named *The Bristol*.

In the absence of his son from Bristol and company affairs, Elias and his grandsons ran the business during most of 1879 when Edward I was shooting alligators in Florida and sightseeing in Europe. Speaking of his grandfather, Edward Ingraham II comments: "Why did Edward I go to Europe in 1879? Health, health, health. He worried about his health from 1857 until he died in 1892. Perhaps he had to."

Though traveling most of 1879, Edward I was in Bristol long enough to induce Patrick Barry of Southington to come to work for Ingrahams. Barry had perfected a method of successfully enameling wood. For more than two decades there was a tremendous demand for such enameled clocks, and at the height of the style's popularity, 18 ovens for enameling were in use. Other clock case companies using the Barry process had to obtain and pay for a license from the Ingrahams.

Edward II recalled:

This black enameled wood goblet was given to me by my father, W. S. Ingraham. He told me that it gave his father, Edward I, the inspiration to go into the black enameled wood case clock business. Edward Ingraham I received a patent for his method of enameling parts to make a clock case. Known as "blacks" or "black enameled mantle clocks." Doubtless Ingraham made several millions of these as they supplied more than 300,000 of one model to the American Tobacco Company.

On October 1, 1875, Edward I's assessment was for $4,255; Elias' for $5,165; and E. Ingraham and Company for $30,000, the last comprising two houses, four factories and $19,000 in investments and mechanical manufacturing operations. These assessments remained static for the next four or five years.

The Bristol National Bank was founded in 1875, later called The Bristol Bank and Trust Company. (Now called "United Bank & Trust Company.") Edward Ingraham I was one of its founders; years later Walter and William Ingraham would be among its directors. After 1920 Edward II and Dudley Ingraham, great-grandsons of Elias, succeeded Walter and William. Elias did not at once open a personal account there, but the Ingraham Company did. Sardonically, from the first ledger it appears that the Ingraham account was consistently overdrawn and on one occasion showed a handsome balance of $2.65. Even so, the Company credit was good. Cash being scarce, many of its transactions of necessity were in barter, finished clocks often were exchanged for needed component parts of wood, metal, glass and paper.

In 1966 among the papers found by Faith Ingraham Treadway was a $50 promissory note dated September 12, 1876, from her father, William Ingraham, to the Ingraham Company. Mrs. Treadway with pride pointed to the reverse side of the note which recorded four equal payments of $12.50 promptly made by her father. Elias' grandson, William Ingraham, was a chip off the old block.

William Ingraham at 19 began at five cents per hour,

a 57-year career with the family clock company. Like Walter, entering the business through nepotism in March, 1876, William was among about 100 employees. As we have seen, the company was not in a particularly strong financial position following the panic of 1873. After three years in the factory, on May 1, 1879, William entered the company office to assist his grandfather, father and older brother, Walter. He was treasurer and general manager from 1900–1930, and contributed markedly to the prosperity and growth of the company.

Though Walter did not attend college, William was for two years a member of the Cornell class of 1878. When under ten, he had been frightfully homesick at boarding school in Stamford, Connecticut. Well educated with an aristocratic bearing and blessed with good health, William also was a born traveler. He traveled to Africa, Alaska, South America, Hawaii, Russia, making eight trips to Europe after 1900. One of his idiosyncracies was traveling with insufficient money in his pocket. On his honeymoon when returning from Niagara Falls, he had to pawn his gold watch to procure railroad tickets from New York City to Bristol.

Vigorous, pink-cheeked, bewhiskered, later in life patriarchal in appearance, William with an erect carriage was an inveterate walker. Bristolites set their clocks by him as he punctually strolled from home to office and return. A man of absolute integrity, thoroughly respected, keen of judgment with natural executive ability, taciturn yet socially inclined, he had a large circle of friends and maintained the high standards of thought and deed inherited from his acquisitive father, Edward I and his avant-garde grandfather, Elias Ingraham.

On July 24, 1878, 24-year-old Walter Ingraham married plain Amelia Fenn of Plymouth, Connecticut, the daughter of a prominent judge. To this union were born four sons. However, the able sons of William, Edward II

Harvest Years

and Dudley, carried the mantle of Ingraham management into mid-20th century. Walter celebrated his 59th wedding anniversary. He died at age eighty-three in 1938 while William lived to the age of seventy-three, passing on in 1930. At his death, Walter was Ingraham board chairman, having retired as president in 1927.

For many years in Bristol the Dunbar factory bell rang ninety-nine times heralding the nine o'clock curfew. For the Ingrahams, going home in the dark was not easy. There was no street lighting except where a few prosperous civic-minded folk set out lamp posts in front of their houses. At night they were apt to bump into the hitching post before every home or fall into a rain puddle. Except for 300 feet of tar path on Main Street in front of the Wallace Barnes Company they walked on dirt sidewalks. In 1876 the telephone was just emerging. William Ingraham later owned the first one in Bristol. Hand pump engine and hose cart were hauled by galloping horses to combat fires. No fire of any consequence threatened the Ingraham Company during the remainder of Elias' lifetime.

In the Yale University Library is a "letter press book" of 1,000 pages of Ingraham Company letters and orders written between January 1, 1878, and June 2, 1882. The bulk of the letters was written in long hand by Edward I and his sons still in their twenties. One to a Brazilian in French was written by Edward I; Elias signed a few as active president of the company. Several times promissory notes rely on the endorsement of Andrew Ingraham, brother still in name and fact to Elias. Andrew's affairs were sound, he was still generous; his substance still backed the Ingraham Company even though nominally he may not have had a financial interest in it. To what extent dear Andrew's support kept the thriving clock company moving forward is conjectural but it must have been relevant, albeit typically unobtrusive as was Andrew's way.

Throughout the "letter press book" is evidence of trading clocks for commodities as well as a continuing shortage of cash. Business was done generally on four months' time. For a period Ingrahams drew drafts on their customers as the company was acutely and chronically short of cash. By the end of 1882 the company cash position improved and some accounts were paid by check. The Ingraham Company constantly bought brass springs, etc., from suppliers in exchange for clocks. There was evidence of some competitors copying Elias' patented designs such as the Venetian and Ionic, and correspondence particularly with the Ansonia Clock Company is of considerable interest. Apparently there was constant trouble with Ansonia which, Ingraham informed a Brazilian customer, on November 1, 1880, "burned to the ground last week." However, the next year Ansonia was back in business giving Ingrahams more headaches.

Correspondence was held with F. Kroeber Clock Company of New York City, with whom Ingrahams was on most friendly terms, also with the American Clock Company and Daniel Pratt and Sons, "All three have been considered by some to be manufacturers but the correspondence does not lend credence to that belief," says Edward Ingraham II.

The earliest Ingraham catalogue known is that of 1881, copies of which are in the Yale library and in the American Clock and Watch Museum. Ingraham published catalogues prior to 1881 but none has been found. (The earliest known illustrated catalogue published by Ingraham is that of 1879. In 1965 the American Clock & Watch Museum published a reprint of the illustrated catalogue of 1881 in which they stated that at that time it was the earliest then known, says Edward Ingraham II.)

The Ingrahams took great pride in the fact that in 1878

all but three of their employees signed the temperance pledge and wore the blue ribbon. The company boasted that "these three are going to sign."

In an editorial of the Bristol *Press* the following appeared:

> Had anyone predicted ten days ago that Bristol would or could be aroused to such a pitch of enthusiasm on the subject of temperance, as now prevails, he would have been thought an idiot. This phlegmatic old town has actually got waked up, and blue ribbon badges are seen on almost everybody's watch chain or lapel.

On April 18, 1878, the *Press* added: "Upwards of 1600 have signed the pledge and wear the blue ribbon"; on April 25, 1878, the *Press* announced that 2,000 people had signed the pledge. This was remarkable when you consider the population of the town at that time was 5,347. Elias and Andrew were teetotalers. This tradition eroded beginning with Edward I and his sons.

In 1880 Elias Ingraham was in his 75th year. The clock company which he founded was already a half century old. It had been hurt by three national depressions, undergone two bankruptcies and a fire, survived a Civil War, moved forward through crises of competition and under-capitalization, marketed hundreds of thousands of clocks of scores of styles throughout the world. Elias witnessed his son Edward I and his grandsons, Walter and William skillfully managing and directing the clock company affairs. Success and fulfillment were now clearly his. Perhaps forgotten were the birth throes when he had mothered, then reared the infant clock company. Before him stood, mature and imposing a full-grown company destined to bloom for generations to come. The remaining five years of his life added more to his comfort, tranquility, and resources.

17

The Pendulum Slows

1880-1884

No pain, no balm; no thorns, no thrones; no gall, no glory; no cross, no crown.

—Penn

Probably the first Connecticut clockmaker to mass produce clocks with American-made springs, Deacon Elisha Brewster, Elias' and Andrew's partner from 1844 to 1852, was "carried off," as Benjamin Franklin would say. The name Brewster and Ingrahams would be known so long as horologists live. It is certain that both Elias and Andrew were saddened by the loss of their venerable partner, who retired as a clockmaker in 1855, the year the Ingraham plant was destroyed by fire.

Noah S. Brewster was his father's executor. It will be remembered that it was Noah's irresponsibility that disrupted and terminated in 1853 the otherwise successful and prosperous Brewster and Ingraham Company.

According to the Funk Funeral Parlor Records, among the funeral expenses Noah paid for his father were: casket, $65; shroud, $4; hearse, $5.

Deacon Brewster's $19,397.25 appraised estate of 1880, though about one-fourth of Elias Ingraham's estate at

The Pendulum Slows

his death in 1885, was nevertheless a tidy legacy, equivalent to more than a quarter of a million dollars in mid-twentieth century inflated values. The clock business was good to Elisha Brewster as it was and would be to Ingrahams for generations to come.

Dropping the sign "&" in 1884, already a living monument to Elias Ingraham, the E. Ingraham Company was incorporated. It became one of the largest manufacturers of clocks and watches in the world. In this new corporation Elias was president, Edward I, general manager. In 1880 a joint stock company had been formed with a capital stock of $100,000. Walter A. Ingraham and William S. Ingraham were admitted to the company at that time. Elias had given Walter $10,000 Ingraham Company stock, while Edward I had given William $5,000 worth. Elias afterward gave William a matching $5,000 making the share of his two grandsons equal. We shall presently see Elias' impartiality, though he had misgivings when he made an Ingraham stock gift to his third grandson, the capricious and errant Irving. Since the age of three Walter Ingraham lived with his grandparents, Elias and Julia.

At the time of his father's death in 1885, Edward I subscribed for the following magazines: *Century; Harper's; Christian Union; Country Gentleman; North American Review;* and *St. Nicholas*. In 1885 Edward I sent *Christian Union* to his daughter Maude, *Century* to William, and *Harper's Bazaar* to Walter. Considering Elias' limited formal education in his boyhood, it is unlikely that he was as catholic a reader as were his better educated son and grandchildren. Occasioned by Elias' financial success, in one or two generations the Ingrahams rose from the provincial to the patrician, from the marginally literate to the liberally lettered and from limited agrarianism to provisional opulence.

In the '80s under Edward I's direction, the Ingraham Company reached one of its most prosperous periods. As Elias was still the leading American clock designer, the company moved forward as a result of his acumen, after its establishment by his talent, tenacity, and temperance. In 1880 the Ingrahams adopted a new process called "endosmotic" (marbleizing) (which Webster defines as "passage through a membrane from a region of lower to a region of higher concentration"). This prepared clock case wood is a reproduction of a popular French style gilded, highly polished, and "as durable as iron." Made of southern poplar, or so-called white wood, given a beautiful finish of successive coats of enamel or japan rubbed into a fine polished finish, these black enamel Ingraham mantel clocks dominated the medium-price field for several decades.

In 1883 Elias and Edward I developed and patented a method of enameling wood that made possible production of black enamel and marbleized clocks. These approached in appearance the French black marble clocks but sold at very low prices and were exceedingly popular. They sold especially well in the South. For many years a few thousand of these clocks were produced weekly.

In 1880 a firm in nearby Waterbury was incorporated as the Waterbury Watch Company and the first thousand so-called Waterbury watches were produced. "They were highly desirable except for the fact they would not run," said Greeley in his history of clocks and watches. However, the fault in the brass wheels was corrected in the next lot. Having 58 parts, a nine-foot mainspring, requiring unlimited winding, the watch was built to sell for $3.50 to $4.00. The common jocose byword of the day was, "We come from Waterbury, the land of eternal spring."

The Pendulum Slows

In 1898 the name of the Waterbury Watch Co. was changed to the New England Watch Co. which failed in 1912. In 1914 the New England Watch Co. was sold to Robert H. Ingersoll & Bros. who failed in 1922.

Robert and Charles Ingersoll conceived the idea of a dollar watch which in the twentieth century became a great seller even by the Ingraham Company. Watches were not made by Ingrahams during Elias' lifetime.

The June 7, 1880, census shows Andrew age 72, a widower, working in a clock shop with two months' unemployment during the current year. His housekeeper was Elizabeth King, 22, his single niece. Elias was listed as 74, a manufacturer living with his wife Julia, 73, who was "keeping house;" still in the Elias Ingraham household, was Walter Ingraham, 25, married, a bookkeeper, having a baby son and a 24-year-old wife Amelia, whose "father was born in England," and a servant, a 17-year-old Irish girl, Marguerite Fluson.

On October 11, 1881, William Ingraham married Grace Ella Seymour, a sister of George Dudley Seymour, whom we have already seen as the documentor of Elias' trip to Caracas in the roaring '40's. Grace Ingraham was a regent in the Daughters of the American Revolution, a church, community, and Red Cross worker, an outstanding woman. In sympathy with the fashion of the day, she did not believe in women's social drinking, though her husband served wine at the Sunday dinner table. In 1890 William Ingraham built a pretentious frame and shingle house later to be occupied by his younger son, Dudley S. Ingraham, who in 1965 gave it to the Connecticut Congregational Missionary Society.

On the occasion of Elias' 79th birthday, Elias wrote to his attentive granddaughter-in-law Grace Ingraham:

Cottage City Oct 1st 1884

Dear Grace

Your letter of the 29th is just at hand covering a Big black Bowe long to be remembered with many thanks for your good wishes and Ice cream. I am glad that Grand Mom is so well and lively and that you all are enjoying your selves so nicely. Remember me in kindness to Mrs. Wistern for waiting on my Dear Wife to such long nice ride. To night I shall enjoy that large dish of Ice cream . . . I don't realize that I am older than a year ago. I am feeling first rate and am enjoying my self nicely. The weather is and has been very fine ever since I came down here. Much more so then in the month of July and their is no ways to disturb my repose. Give my love to Wife and all of our dear friends.

Your Affectionate Grand Father
Elias Ingraham

Here is another example in Elias and Julia's married life where he traveled or vacationed without her, a point perhaps indicating his rather than her adventuresome spirit, even at 79.

Doubtless Elias rejoiced at his grandson's choice of a wife, for Grace Ingraham was a thoughtful, virtuous, and talented woman as may be seen by this eulogy 44 years later.

Using the text, "man goeth forth unto his work, unto his labor until the evening," Psalm 104:23, Rev. Ernest L. Wismer, Pastor of the First Congregational Church at Bristol, Connecticut, on April 26, 1925, preached an appropriate funeral sermon.

> In her friendships, Mrs. Ingraham gave herself so freely, and she had so much to give. Richly endowed in mind and heart with a ripe culture gained through wide reading and travel, gifted with a nature keenly sensitive to the

finest in art and literature, and passionately fond of music, she found opportunities everywhere of the enriching of her life . . . . She was so responsive to the beautiful that I wonder whether this is not the reason that we could never think of her as being old. Her interests were always so fresh and vivid, and she found such joy in life because life was to her so full of beauty. Her spirit mellowed but did not age with the years because she never lost her capacity to appreciate the revelations of beauty granted to her.

I have never known one who could help others with a finer tact and a nobler considerateness of the feelings of the recipient. Like Mary, who broke the box of alabaster ointment over the Master, so our dear friend knew how to put into some deed that tender insight that made it the disclosure of her own nature.

The deepest aspect of her nature was her Christian faith. Her quiet confidence in the divine Father, and her lifelong devotion to the Master suggest the sources of her poise and self-control, her fine balance of character, and her unwearied kindness . . . . Her relations with God were as natural and as spontaneous as with her famliy or her friends. And so at the close, when she knew that she was going, her hope in that larger life was steadfast. She had an anchor within the veil, and she knew it would hold. She had no fear, and she passed on like a noble vessel that seeks its harbor and final rest.

When the first publication of the Bristol *Press* appeared in 1871, there was no central water supply in Bristol. Although there were a few pipe lines from private springs, more than half the town depended upon wells. The "Chic Sales" type of outdoor architecture was a feature of every home site; therefore, it is not hard to visualize the typhoid epidemics that regularly visited the town. For several years after the *Press* commenced publication, editorials such as these frequently appeared:

"Typhoid fever had made its appearance in town, and through the fall, as usual, there will probably be many cases. Foul gases and overwork are to be avoided. If they are, the cases will be fewer than otherwise."

"There seems to be numerous cases of typhoid fever in town, and some deaths have been occasioned by it. Clean premises, thorough ventilation and plenty of rest are the best safeguards."

If one is surprised that the *Press* was so naive, it is well to remember that it had been published for six years before the brilliant French scientist, Louis Pasteur, established the germ theory. The severity of these annual typhoid visitations would have been worse had it not been that a few privately-owned spring lines covered a considerable part of the town.

On December 27, 1883, the *Press* carried the following article:

> A petition will be presented to the legislature at its coming session for the incorporation of a company to be known as the Bristol Water Company, with power to take water from the south part of Burlington, near the residence of Ira B. Taft, to construct such dams and reservoirs in Burlington and Bristol as may be necessary to bring the water into the village of Bristol, and to lay pipes where needful . . . .

Although September 10 was the day of the completion of the Bristol water works, water had been delivered in part of the system three months earlier. June 17, 1885 was a most appropriate day and year to get water as Bristol was exactly one hundred years old as a town, and at 6:00 A.M. Federal Hill cannon boomed salutes, church bells rang, 10,000 people thronged to hear and see the

The Pendulum Slows

celebration. So it was that a municipal water system was completed in Bristol a few weeks after Elias' death.

As the wood around Bristol was cut down, by the '80s the Pequabuck had decreased to one-fourth of the flow it had held in the day of the first settlement of Bristol. Various small brooks upon which factories depended had almost dried up. The new water system stopped typhoid scourges. The arrival of piped-in water also corresponded with the revolutionary invention known as inside plumbing. All these appeared just as Elias passed beyond the vale.

Among the treasured letters which have come down to this day from Elias in his own handwriting is one dated December 25, 1884, Christmas day. It was Elias and Julia's 57th wedding anniversary. Written to his irresponsible grandson, Irving,

>Bristol Dence 25th 1884
>
>Ervan My Dear Grand Son
> I Present to You this transfir of one hundred share ten thousand Dollars Stock in the E Ingraham & Co Clock Concirn. With this Expres Wish and Expectation that you are to Setle down in life Business and Ucefulness in Church Sosiety and Town. I hope You Will More then Make My place good, or More then fill My place Which I have got to Soon vacate. It's now fifty seven Years this Evening Since I United My Destiny With Julia H Sparks, I then had nothing to start out in life on Except a trade Which I had surved Five Years Apprentice Ship for the Cabinet Business I had Made Contract With Geo Mitchell to Work on Clock Cases one Year for one Dollar and twenty five cents Per Day And twelve hours for a Days Work. Our Boys would think such a prospect prety hard woud they Not. To Suppurte one self and Wife But as God in whom I trust has Blest us in our union and in our Business and we have lived happyly to ge ther this fifty

Seven years and have attained to our present Security and Now I Want this Clock Business to be kept and continued in the Hands and Harts of the Ingrahams Family for Many Generations to Come.

Your Affectionate Grand Father
Elias Ingraham

Elias' "express Wish and Expectation" that "Ervan" "Setle down in life and Business and ucefulness in Church and Sosiety and Town" sounds almost like an order, but one which fell on deaf ears. Did Elias' hope that Irving would "More then fill My place which I have got to Soon vacate" portend an imminent declination? Did Elias have an omen of his own demise or was he merely indicating his prospective retirement as president of the Ingraham Company? Combining thoughts of baccalaureate and valedictory, Elias' unselfish desire for his posterity was, "Now I want this Clock Business to be kept and continued in the Hands and Harts of the Ingrahams Family for Many Generations to Come." By late 1967 his clock business, while no longer exclusively kept in Ingraham hands, nevertheless continued in Ingraham hearts into a seventh generation, fulfilling his hope "For Many Generations to Come."

The family character on the male side was George Dudley Seymour, Mrs. William Ingraham's brother, while on the distaff side it was Anna Anthofer Ingraham, Irving's wife. Anna and Irving were married in London, July 21, 1893, the year following Edward I's death. Anna had a child. However, she and Irving would be childless. Anna's son, Arthur Anthofer, as an adult adopted the surname, Ingraham. Later his three wives and the three daughters they bore also took the name Ingraham though they were not of that bloodline. Arthur, according to all reports from Austria, was considered to be Anna's illegitimate son, sired by Emperor Franz Joseph. If not by the Emperor himself, then by one of his court. Anna, an attractive girl of 16, had been rewarded for her favored imprudence with a lovely home in the country which she called *Einsiedelei,* "The Hermitage." Later Anna told Arthur, then a long-haired musician, to keep away from her and Irving's home in Los Angeles. She disinherited him and he passed out of the Ingraham story in ignominy.

18

Wingspread!

1885

It is time to be old, to take in sail.
—Emerson

For more than four score years the clock plant on Elias Ingraham's one-and-one-half acre corner flourished. It is now the 58th year of his and Julia's marriage. See their Farmington Avenue, two-story, shingled roofed home with outhouse and barn behind. It is midsummer. Fine old New England hardwoods and shrubs, well foliated, abound along the side road, Burlington Avenue. Andrew Ingraham's home is across there.

Let us go up the steps onto the front porch facing nearly south, lift the heavy knocker and await the greeting of our esteemed Yankee clockmaker. Elias and Julia, young no more (he nearly eighty, she seventy-eight), greet us with typical New England reserve though with gracious hospitality.

We observe Elias, tall, large-framed, imposing, quiet, unassuming, affable, kindly, generous, dignified.

We enter the dim, high-ceilinged downstairs hallway with carpeted wood floor, mahogany table with candleholder, hat rack, hair cloth chairs, portraits of both Elias

Wingspread!

and Julia in their thirties, painted by an itinerant unnamed artist.

There, leading up, are carpeted stairs with carved balustrade. Feel the atmosphere of modest elegance, quiet assurance and well ordered lives. Much of this furniture was made by Elias himself, as of course were the handsome shelf clocks of living lumber heard striking the hour throughout the house.

Just off the hall is the spacious, carpeted, comfortable sitting room furnished with secretary and bookcase filled with books, the well read family Bible with vital statistics, hair cloth sofa and chair, oil lamp, five rocking chairs, marble-top table. The walls are papered, the draperies drawn. Note the unmistakable scent of humid woodwork in a Connecticut midsummer.

Step now into the darkened carpeted double parlor with sliding doors between, furnished with eleven handsome black walnut period chairs in red upholstery, two rockers, two more marble-topped tables with candlesticks, an elegant long gilt mirror on the wall, a Hazelton piano that their son, Edward I, plays when visiting them.

Walking through the light and airy carpeted dining room, observe the dozen oak chairs with cane seats, the dining table with extensions covered with crocheted doilies, bureau and another bookcase against the wall, chair rail, fancy settee near the window. See in your mind's eye a dinner or supper held here with abstemious Ingraham friends or family, unstimulated by any personality adjustment from spirituous imbibing.

Just off the dining room we look into the kitchen, Julia's daily abode, with cupboards filled with crockery, table wear, pots and pans. There is the pantry well stocked with flour, sugar, and home-grown potatoes, ice box, butter churn, a wood burning iron cook stove, brick flue, wood box filled with neatly stacked split stovewood, sink and drainboard with hand pump from the cistern, modest kitchen furniture of a well-used extension table covered with oil cloth, with four sturdy chairs where the Ingrahams breakfasted across from each other for so long.

Just off the kitchen lies a small uncarpeted tenant's room with bedstead, stand, and a pair of chairs where a hired girl or man stays.

Ascending the stairs off the entry hall, now enter the spacious carpeted upper hall, furnished with four hair cloth chairs, a large stand, oak cupboard and chest with drawers, and a large trunk at the far end under a window.

Off the upstairs hall lie four large, high-ceilinged, carpeted bedrooms. In both the front right and back right chambers, see handsome eleven-piece black walnut period bedroom sets, in the front left and back left chambers eight-piece sets, one black walnut, the other painted, with an air-tight stove in the former. In the latter room are four sets of chamber crockery, table cloths, spreads and towels, four extra beds, three hair mattresses, bedding and three feather beds.

Outside, past woodshed and well, stroll to the barn. Indicating the scope of small farm husbandry, observe inside a hoe, rake, manure fork, scoop shovel, chopping axe for firewood, crowbar, bush cutter, two round-point shovels, draft chains, three hay rakes and four forks, two spades, potato hook, iron wedges for splitting wood, scythe and swath grain cradle.

Hear the two milk cows lowing softly, the hog grunting indignantly; notice a handsome span of red oxen grazing in the adjoining fifteen-acre meadow; see a silent ox cart with wooden yoke, a plow, a harrow. Peer at the loft where stored are fifty bushels of apples from the orchard, a dozen bushels of home-grown potatoes, ear corn for the pig, twenty-three bushels of rye, seven tons of fragrant loose hay, just stowed. Even in their autumnal days, Elias

Wingspread!

and Julia's rural roots remain to sprout through their urban affluence.

Elias' estate would be presently inventoried by probate court appraisers Lewis and Beckwith at more than $93,000 —equal to more than a million dollars in purchasing power of the 1970s.

Elias Ingraham had accumulated from his thrift, energy and talent, a modest fortune. Additionally he had bestowed much substance to his son and three grandsons which would last for generations to come.

In his eightieth year, Elias yet looked forward:

> Elias Ingraham contemplates laying out his meadow land near his house into building lots in the spring. He will continue the road already commenced, near the case factory, running east to the street, running north past his residence, and coming out opposite the house of Andrew Ingraham. This will open a number of fine lots and no doubt they will find a ready sale!
> (From the Bristol *Press* of January 8, 1885)

Elias' proposed meadow subdivision was preempted by a terminal incident in the late summer of 1885 at Martha's Vineyard.

The dean of 19th century American clock designers, Elias had kept the Ingraham Company like a talisman among the leaders of the clock industry for decades. As evidence of this, during the week of June 13, 1885, at a Bristol Centennial, seventy-two of the better known among the hundreds of Elias' clock designs were exhibited. One was designed for George Mitchell dated 1835, another designed for C. and L. C. Ives in 1840, an 1845 Gallery clock; Round, Sharp, and Column Gothics, Papier Mâché, Venetian, Doric, Grecian, Ionic, Centennial, Oriental, Dragon, Acme, O.K., Phoenix, Halcyon, Cadet, Lotus, Alpine, Paladin, Annex, Parisian, Peerless, Index,

Dixie, Decade, Expert, Nabob, Graphic, Monograph, Faultless, Princess, Black Prince, Eclipse, Bonardgo, Basilisk, Liberty, Niagara, Star, Dauntless, Maxim, Postal, Crayon, Ingraham Calendar, Dew Drop Calendar, Brazil, Reflector, Iota, Arcade, Era, Crystal, Round and Corrugated Gallery. All these clock designs and nine hundred more had welled up out of the fertile Ingraham reservoir—clocks that ticked and timed and chimed around the globe in homes occidental and oriental.

A picture of Elias taken at this Centennial shows him in a stiff collar, and then fashionable tie, standing erect behind the exhibit of his clocks. He has abundant white hair, full beard, dark eyebrows, long nose, thin face, high forehead, mouth a little turned down at the corners.

Edward Ingraham II says of this picture, "There is shown a telephone beside the clocks. I assume the Ingrahams were proud to exhibit that modern communications tool!"

Following the week of his clock exhibit, about August 1, Elias for the last time sought out, as was his custom in the summertime, the island retreat at Martha's Vineyard. There during the heated period, he stayed in his Gothic cottage, enjoyed the cooling sea breezes from off the Atlantic, walked paths among deep summer verdure, combed the beach, peered skyward at sea fowl and clouds, scanned the ocean, and watched passing ships now mostly steam, though still with some sail.

Undoubtedly he contemplated his life so fully lived, a family both responsible and appreciative and business born as it were like a baby in a manger but now established as a thriving, internationally known adult company.

Likely his modesty would not admit of the esteem and respect that he both earned and received from his peers. While it is certain he loved the sunrise, perhaps we could forgive him now for more affinity with the island sunsets,

Wingspread! 211

for his career and life on this planet were like the orb of day descending towards evening soon to disappear beyond the vale. His thoughts drifted toward his obscure boyhood at the Marlborough Farm before 1822 with father and mother and Andrew, his apprentice years at Glastonbury, his acquaintance there with Julia and their subsequent marriage in 1827, his year in Hartford with Daniel Dewey, the seventeen-mile walk with George Warren to Bristol in May fifty-eight years before, his exciting clock design contract with George Mitchell, his partnerships with the Ives and others in the early 1830s, the coming of his faithful brother to Bristol, his high expectation and disappointment with the patented invalid chair, the panic of 1837, his gloomy bankruptcy of 1840, the exotic trip to South America, the Brewster and Ingrahams successful partnership until 1853, the catastrophic fire of 1855, the second trying bankruptcy of 1857, the salvaging of scorched lumber from the fire and the reinstatement of the clock company therefrom, business struggles during the lean Civil War years and after, partnership with his sons and grandsons, the trip to California in 1873, Ingraham Company prosperity during most of the 1870s and early 1880s, misgivings concerning his grandson Irving's vacillation, the multiple joys and peace of this Martha's Vineyard Paradise, contemplations of the hereafter and its traditional theology of reward for work well done.

Surely he mused on that expressed hope in his valedictory the Christmas before to "Dear Ervan,"

> . . . Now I want this clock business to be kept and continued in the hands and harts of the Ingrahams family for many generations to come . . . .

About to be taken away, he could not know how well his hope was to be fulfilled, for the clock business indeed would be kept for generations to come in both the hands and hearts of the Ingraham family.

That the family already was doing fairly well may be seen from these tax assessments of October 1, 1885: Andrew Ingraham, grand list, $1,200; Edward I, grand list, $5,265; Irving, grand list $50, taxed 75 cents plus $2 military commutation; Walter, grand list $2,625; taxed $39.88 including a military commutation; William, grand list $1,515 taxed $22.73 with a military commutation; E. Ingraham Company, grand list $29,000 taxed $435 on seven mills, stores, and manufactures valued at $14,000 and investments in mechanical and manufacture operations of $15,000; Julia, a widow of six weeks at the time of this assessment, showed a grand list of $8,275 taxed $124.13 on three houses, sixteen acres, two neat cattle, along with bank, insurance and manufactures stock.

In spite of his grandfather's frequent remonstrances, Irving with a grand list of $50 was inclined to be harum-scarum.

The prosperity of the Ingraham Company may be seen from the profits made from 1872 through 1885 to wit: 1872, $4,500; 1873, the year of Elias' California trip, $36,890; 1874, $450 showing the influence from the panic of 1873; 1875, $13,720; 1876, $10,800; 1877, loss of $1,960; 1878, loss of $9,340; 1879, $1,350; 1880, $18,700; 1881, loss of $5,400; 1882, $18,560; 1883, $8,468; 1884, $31,186; and the year of Elias' death, 1885, $38,510.

The clock company in the 13 last years of Elias' life netted the tidy sum of $166,434 which must be multiplied 10 to 20 times to conceive of it in terms of present buying power.

The end came for Elias Ingraham at his cottage in Martha's Vineyard in 1885. The Waterbury *Daily American* on August 18, 1885 carried this notice of his passing:

> The remains of Elias Ingraham are expected to arrive from Martha's Vineyard tonight at 7:20. Mr. and Mrs.

Edward Ingraham were there at the time of his death, and after their arrival to-day, arrangements will be made for the funeral which, it is hoped, will be held in the Congregational Church on account of the large number desirous of attending. It is expected that the Rev. H. T. Staats of Glastonbury, the recent pastor of the Congregational Church here, will officiate. Mr. Ingraham was 79 last October, and when he went away the 1st of July, seemed to possess unusual vigor for a man of his age and had just completed his notes for the history of the clock manufacturing in Bristol, with which he has been intimately connected for the last 50 years and probably had done more in bringing out elegant designs for cases which appeared in the exhibit of the E. Ingraham Co. at the late centennial. The shop of the Ingraham Co. closed last night till after the funeral and contributions were made by the employees for a floral tribute to the memory of the deceased. The remains were placed in a metallic casket and the funeral will probably occur Thursday.

And on August 20, 1885, the Waterbury *Daily American* noted: Mr. and Mrs. W. S. Ingraham arrived Wednesday morning from Lake George, having spent some time in the Catskills. He received a telegram at the former place announcing the death of his grandfather and made a continuous journey by team and rail, reaching here by the 9 o'clock train.

The Hartford *Times* in that month and year noted:

Mr. Elias Ingraham, the head of the well known clock manufacturing firm known as the E. Ingraham Company, of Bristol, died of cholera morbus at his summer residence at Cottage City, Martha's Vineyard last Sunday, and was buried at Bristol on Thursday. Mr. Ingraham was one of the pioneers in the clock making industry, which has added so largely to the building up of Connecticut as a manufacturing state, and for many years the Ingraham Company has been noted far and wide for the excellent quality of the goods it produces. One of their clocks hangs in the composing room of the Times and for years has served faithfully to regulate the various operations necessary in getting the several editions to press.

Personally, Mr. Ingraham was one of the most respected citizens of Bristol. He was for many years a consistent member of the Congregational Church in that town, and took a deep interest in religious and moral concerns. His simple and unassuming manners, and kind and genial disposition, served to attach to him many friends, and by none was he more esteemed than by those in his employ.

Edward Ingraham II writes: "In the hospital I met an old white-haired lady, Mrs. Day. Her father was Scotch and worked at Ingraham Company. She said that he was a bearer at Elias' funeral and very proud of the honor. That he had a 'swallow tail,' and that he wore it as bearer at the funeral which was a great honor and privilege." Could this have been Deacon Day who worked for and with Elias twenty-five or thirty years before?

Augustus Funk found this clipping in his funeral parlor file, apparently from the Bristol *Press:*

Death has again come and taken one of our aged and highly esteemed citizens, Elias Ingraham. Mr Ingraham went some weeks ago, as his custom has been for several years, to spend the heated term at Cottage City, Martha's Vineyard. There, about a fortnight ago, he was seized with cholera morbus, and the disease was of so violent a nature that it baffled the skill of physicians, and he died at 4:30 o'clock last Sunday afternoon. His remains reached here Tuesday evening, and the funeral occurs to-day at 2 o'clock at his late residence, Rev. Mr. Staats officiating . . . .

According to the *World Book Encyclopedia,* "Cholera morbus is a condition which usually occurs in hot weather.

It is caused by chemical poisoning, sudden chilling of the intestinal tract, or by food which is infected by a number of bacteria."

The terminal illness was sudden, extreme and brief. Was Julia with him or was she in Bristol? It would appear she was not with him although Edward I and his wife were there when the unhappy end came. Elias' grandson, William, and his wife were vacationing, first in the Catskills in southern New York then at Lake George in upstate New York. There they received the melancholy intelligence. In the absence from the Ingraham factories of Elias, Edward I and William it is likely that Walter, perhaps even Irving, was "minding the store" in Bristol. There they learned of their esteemed grandfather's death.

After the funeral Elias' remains were interred in the Ingraham plot in Bristol's three-acre West Cemetery founded in 1836, the year Andrew Ingraham came to Bristol. Inexplicably the headstone states 1886 as the year of Elias' death. Of course, it was 1885.

Elias left no will. Neither would Edward I leave a will at his death. Much of Elias' furniture later came to Irving and Anna Ingraham though Anna returned some of it to some Bristol Ingrahams.

Is there not a time for mortals to be born, a time for them to die, seasons for everything? If earth be a preparatory school you, Elias Ingraham, designer, and maker of clocks, husband, father, brother, beloved citizen, you have graduated magna cum laude. To yourself have you ascended, while to us you are buried?

Beyond mortal view, beyond earth's thrall, sing, Elias, sing with the heavenly choir as now the notes of the bell in the meeting house steeple sound a melancholy requiem for those near and dear at graveside. To Ingraham posterity, the notes ring out an anthem, a hymn of richer, fuller lives for those yet earthbound.

For threescore years you, Elias, labored, won and lost, won and lost again, hoping that your life work would enure to the benefit of your family for generations to come. It has. How well it comes true, perchance you know not, neither suspect. We, yet earthbound, undergraduates of our own preparatory school, are uplifted by your persistence and pluck. We recall your trudging to Bristol from Hartford with metal tools of craft on your back and mental tools of survival in your heart. Both worked wondrously well. The plane, the saw, the compass, the chisel on your back supplement the courage, the patience, the talent in your leonine character during an eighty-year lifetime of trial and victories.

Lest discouragement overwhelm or confidence undercut, it is well that Providence withheld its transcript until your life was swung pendulum-like a day at a time through the midnights as well as noontides of your destiny.

Not an historian, yet you made history . . . not an epicurean, yet you were a tastemaker—a man of action rather than sound, courage rather than sentiment, reality rather than fancy, with qualities that were not emotions but engrained ways of life, a paragon culled through tribulation as gold is screened from dross through the sieve of experience. You brought to Bristol tools sharp of hand and mind, leaving an example of uncommon manhood. For the nation you are a lesson in industry. To Bristol and Ingrahams, you left a company destined to survive and prosper beyond your kin.

"You departed this life wound up in the hope of being taken in hand by your Maker and of being thoroughly cleaned and repaired and set agoing in the world to come."

Epilogue

Elias Ingraham began his company with little more than pluck. He left it with five factories employing more than 500 people who manufactured 250,000 clocks annually.

In 1887, two years after Elias' death, the Ingraham Company increased its capital from $100,000 to $250,000 in stock held by Edward Ingraham I and his three sons.

In August of that year the capricious Irving Ingraham, then 27, was placed in charge of the movement division upon the retirement of Anson Atwood. Irving held the position until 1892, the year of his father Edward I's untimely death. It seemed odd that Edward's obituary made no mention of his mother. Bewidowed Julia Ingraham, though she was still living at the time of the death of her only child, always seemed to have taken a back seat.

Andrew died in 1894 at the age of 87, after suffering from cancer of the nose. Andrew's will declared: "I commend my soul to God and my body back to its original dust Amen."

To the very last, Andrew remained pious, unselfish and considerate. His bequests to missionary and Bible societies indicated his affection for, and responsibility to, religious affairs.

By the mid-1960s, out of 400 original clock companies

in and around Bristol, only two remained—Ingraham and Sessions.

Management of the Ingraham Company had continued successfully with Walter and William Ingraham (1892–1927) followed by Edward Ingraham II (1927–1954), and his brother Dudley Ingraham (1954–1956).

After Dudley Ingraham's retirement as president, the office was held for the first time by non-Ingrahams in the sequence of Robert Cooper (1956–1961), Bret Neece (1961–1963), and W. A. Songer (1963–1967). In the company's 136th year on October 20, 1967, a special meeting of Ingraham stockholders was held in the Parish Hall of The First Congregational Church of Bristol. The sale of the Ingraham Company was overwhelmingly approved by a 99.996 majority and without dissent to McGraw-Edison.

It was fitting that the sale of Elias Ingraham's company in 1967 was approved on the property of the Bristol Congregational Church where in 1832 Elias and other church members erected a colonial meeting house that still stands in original beauty and grace.

Thus it was that a company founded in 1831 by Elias Ingraham and under lineal family management for a century and a third was sold to a large corporation.

The hope of Elias Ingraham on Christmas Day, 1884, his 57th wedding anniversary, was fulfilled beyond his sanguine expectations. That was the day on which he wrote his grandson the quaint line stating his wishes: "Now I want this Clock Business to be kept and continued in the Hands and Harts of the Ingrahams Family for Many Generations to Come."

For their work continueth . . .
Broad and deep . . .
Greater than their knowing

Index

American Clock and Watch Museum   20, 56, 88, 138, 163, 194
American Coal Barge Company   172
Ansonia, Conn.   153, 154, 155, 160, 189, 194

B. Aymar & Co.   17
Barber, Gideon, Jr.   102
Barber, Rhoda   102
Barnes Family   56, 72, 119, 152, 172, 189, 193
Barnum, P. T.   86, 88
Barr and Buell   150
Bartholomew, George   177
Bartholomew, William   90
Beach, Eliza Jane   144, 148
Beach, Hammond   144, 155
Beals, Carleton   91
Beckwith, Dana   71
Birge, John   92, 99
Birge, Nathaniel L.   155, 167, 172
Birge's Pond   171
Bishop, Lucy   115
Black Ball Line   45
Boardman, Chauncey   71, 117
Brewster, Elisha C.   29, 71, 72, 84, 89, 93, 105, 108, 117, 120, 136, 144, 145, 146, 173, 196, 197
Brewster and Ingraham   20, 30, 113, 115, 118, 119, 120, 121, 126, 132, 133, 134, 137, 142, 143, 144, 145, 170, 196, 211
Brewster, Noah L.   72, 133, 136, 196
Bristol Bank and Trust Co.   191
Bristol, Conn.   15, 17, 20, 24, 28, 29, 31, 39, 40, 52, 53, 54, 55, 56, 58, 59, 60, 61, 64, 66, 67, 68, 70, 72,

219

73, 79, 80, 83, 86, 87, 88, 89, 93, 96, 97, 98, 99, 100, 102, 105, 106, 107, 111, 117, 121, 122, 126, 132, 133, 134, 140, 142, 145, 146, 151, 153, 154, 155, 157, 158, 159, 160, 162, 171, 173, 176, 177, 180, 187, 189, 193, 206, 213, 214, 215, 216, 218
Bristol Brass Company 142
Bristol Knitting Company 93, 142
Bristol National Bank 191
Bristol *Press* 70, 121, 133, 167, 173, 174, 175, 176, 178, 195, 201, 202, 209, 214
Brown, Jonathan C. 68, 90, 159
Brownson, Daniel 56
Burwell, S. 112

California 163, 170, 174, 175, 176, 177, 179–186, 205, 211
Caracas, Venezuela 16, 20, 22, 23, 24, 25, 29, 31, 108, 116, 121, 122, 125, 126
Carrier Families 32, 33, 34, 38, 40, 115
Cheney, Benjamin 66
Chicago, Ill. 156, 157, 178

Cone, Rev. Jonathan 91
Congregational Church at Bristol, Glastonbury and Marlborough 31, 50, 56, 57, 59, 72, 77, 91, 97, 101, 171, 173, 188, 200, 213, 214, 218

Darrow, Elijah 67, 71
Davis and Barbour 98, 108
Day, William 160, 214
Dewey, Daniel 51, 52, 64, 107
Dickens, Charles 120
Downing, Andrew Jackson 127
Downs, Ephraim 71, 73
Downs, Frank 71
Dunbar, Col. E. L. 152
Dupouy, Walter 20, 22

E. and A. Ingraham Clock Company 148, 150, 151, 153, 154, 164, 171
E. C. Brewster & Co. 116
The E. Ingraham Companies 72, 88, 156, 158, 160, 169, 170, 171, 172, 175, 188, 191, 193, 194, 197, 198, 204, 209, 211, 212, 213, 217, 218
Elizabethtown, Kentucky 43

Index

Farmington Canal 80, 132
Finley, Lucy 93, 101
Fitch, John 66
Forestville, Conn. 55
Franz Joseph, Emperor 204
Funk Families 133, 187, 196, 214

Gilbert, William 172
Gillett, B. C. 52
Glastonbury, Conn. 46, 48, 50, 51, 66, 75, 77, 86, 111, 123, 131, 211
Goodrich, Chauncey 90
Gothic Clocks — Sharp, Round, Arch and Column 11, 17, 20, 26, 27, 28, 29, 30, 119, 122, 123, 124, 125, 126, 129, 131, 133, 136, 156, 159, 166, 209
"Gotion," Indiana 139
Griswold, Rev. Samuel 50
Guilford, Conn. 65, 100, 153, 155, 171

Hale, Nathan 11, 76, 121
Hartford, Conn. 29, 52, 55, 66, 75, 78, 86, 89, 107, 132, 165, 211, 216
Hayes (Benjamin F.) Patent Chair 106, 107, 110, 111, 172

Herendeen, Maude Ingraham 170, 197
Hill, Peter 65
Hinman, Alonzo 52, 69
Holly, Jean T. 21
Howland & Aspenwall 17
Hull, George 57

Indian River, Florida 157, 190
Ingersoll Watch Co. 199
Ingraham and Goodrich 90
Ingraham and Peck 110
Ingraham and Ross 110
Ingrahams and Stedman 151
Ingraham, Andrew 18, 20, 29, 39, 40, 42, 43, 46, 78, 84, 88, 90, 93, 100, 101, 102, 111, 112, 113, 114, 115, 116, 117, 125, 126, 133, 135, 136, 138, 140, 141, 143, 144, 145, 146, 148, 151, 153, 154, 155, 157, 166, 172, 187, 188, 193, 195, 196, 199, 212, 215, 217
Ingraham, Bailey and Co. 94
Ingraham, Edward 7
Ingraham, Edward I 17, 85, 86, 87, 96, 97, 113, 133, 146, 147, 148, 150,

151, 152, 153, 154, 155, 156, 157, 158, 160, 161, 162, 163, 166, 167, 170, 171, 172, 173, 175, 188, 189, 190, 191, 192, 193, 195, 197, 198, 207, 212, 213, 215
Ingraham, Edward II 9, 74, 106, 118, 121, 163, 176, 190, 192, 195, 210, 214, 218
Ingraham, Eliza Jane 144, 155, 161
Ingraham, Dudley S. 145, 191, 193, 199, 218
Ingraham, Honora Sparks Andrew 90, 169, 166, 187
Ingraham, Irving and Anna Anthofer 163, 197, 203, 205, 211, 212, 215, 217
Ingraham, Joseph I and Betty Taylor 40, 90
Ingraham, Joseph II 34, 35, 38, 40, 115
Ingraham, Joseph III and Eunice 34, 39, 40, 41, 42, 43, 78, 157
Ingraham, Julia 15, 17, 24, 26, 30, 31, 46, 57, 85, 90, 94, 120, 122, 124, 133, 144, 148, 164, 166, 167, 172, 175, 197, 199, 203, 206, 207, 209, 211, 215, 217

Ingraham, Nathaniel 40, 59
Ingraham, Richard 34
Ingraham, Rhoda Barber 102, 113, 114, 135, 155, 187
Ingraham, Walter Andrew and Amelia Fenn 156, 157, 158, 161, 166, 167, 171, 175, 176, 191, 192, 193, 195, 197, 199, 212, 215, 218
Ingraham and Warren 74
Ingraham, William S. and Grace Seymour 122, 145, 156, 158, 161, 163, 171, 172, 190, 191, 192, 195, 197, 199, 200, 212, 213, 215, 218
The Ives Families 68, 71, 88, 89, 99, 104, 105, 109, 110, 111, 113, 114, 119

Jerome and Darrow 79, 110
Jerome, Chauncey and Noble 18, 30, 52, 53, 67, 68, 69, 70, 71, 96, 97, 100, 103, 104, 105, 110, 117, 118, 134, 151, 152
Jerome, S. B. 89, 93, 116

Kirk, Charles 120

La Guayra 20, 21, 22, 23, 25, 26

Index 223

Leroy, Anna Marie 65
Loomis, Mr. 71

Mahogany 27, 49, 97, 130, 131, 132, 188
Manross, E. 117
Manross, Nehemiah 56
Marlborough, Conn. 34, 41, 44, 46, 48, 78, 93, 100, 115, 210
Martha's Vineyard 78, 157, 165, 167, 172, 173, 209, 210, 211, 212, 213, 214
Mitchell, George 52, 53, 69, 70, 72, 73, 74, 75, 79, 80, 83, 102, 128, 163, 203, 209, 211
Montenden, Hannah, with Nicollet and Maria 66
Myer, Geller and Fernald 126

New Cambridge, Conn. 56, 58, 59
New Haven Clock Company 123, 153
Norton, Augustin 160
Norton, Frederick Calvin 121
Nutting, Wallace 73

Paez, Jose Antonio 21
Palmer, Brooks 63, 68, 119

Parmele, Ebenezer 65
Patents 159, 160, 163, 164, 171, 172
Peck, Epaphroditus 41, 117, 118, 133, 145
Peck, Joseph 172
Peck, Josiah 107
Peck, Newman 57
Peck, Tracy 71
Pequabuck River 53, 57, 60, 79, 96, 108, 171, 203
Pillar and Scroll Shelf Clock 66, 128
Plymouth, Conn. 66
"Pole-land" 55
Platt, Daniel, Jr. 134, 194

Ray, Benjamin 29, 114, 115, 116, 118, 126, 132, 171
Ray and Ingraham Co. 88, 115, 116, 118, 125
Richards, Alanson 72
Roberts, Gideon 66
Roberts, Hiram, George and Titus 106, 107, 111
Rogers, Isaiah 81, 82

Sessions, J. H. 172
Seymour, George Dudley 11, 28, 121, 122, 124, 199, 204
Sparks family 46, 51, 75, 76, 77, 78, 79, 90, 93, 111, 112, 123

Stedman, Edmund Clarence 147, 148, 151, 152
Stevens, Edward 123
Stocking, Jeremiah 77, 78

Talcott, Samuel 112, 135
Terry Families 66, 67, 86, 105
Thomas, Seth 67
Treadway, Faith Ingraham 188, 191
Treadway, Jean 11
Treadway, Morton C., Sr. 9

Treat, Sherman and Barzillai 96
Tudor, Frederick 134

Waterbury, Conn. 97, 198, 199, 212, 213
Warren, George 51, 74, 85, 86
Watson, Luman 73
Welch, Elisha 160
Welch, George 71

Yale University 64, 87, 146, 148, 151, 193, 194